WHAT PEOPLE ARE SAYING ABOUT

IN JUST

I have known David for o·   .is love
and passion for liturgy has .   ·..ueiit. He understands liturgy
as a missional tool which speaks to people in various ways and at
significant spiritual levels, not least in the Eucharist as it focuses
on the presence of Christ. Being sensitive to contemporary liturgy
and worship, David understands how this has been influenced by
the Prayer Book and why it is important to understand its lasting
impact and relevance in the Church's prevailing culture and
direction. As a theological student, I learnt much about liturgy
from David and I am confident this book will make a valuable
contribution to the reader's understanding and experience of the
Prayer Book, which is a rich inheritance.

The Rt Rev Peter Burrows, Bishop of Doncaster

As the Church in Europe celebrates 500 years of Reformation, the
Church of England is still working out what it means to be
'semper reformanda', embracing both continuity and change.
This is a fascinating take on a key bit of Anglican history by an
experienced parish liturgical practitioner – a sort of liturgical
'whodunit', whose consequences are still being worked out in
the Church today.

The Ven Robert Jones, Archdeacon of Worcester

In Just Three Years is a delightful and comprehensive account of
the formative years of the Book of Common Prayer and how
those three years have continued to influence Anglican liturgy to
the present day. I highly commend this vivid and fascinating
book. The reader is in for a treat!

The Ven Helene T. Steed, Archdeacon of Clogher

In Just Three Years

Pentecost 1549 to All Saints' 1552 –
A Tale of Two Prayer Books

In Just Three Years

Pentecost 1549 to All Saints' 1552 –
A Tale of Two Prayer Books

Canon David Jennings

Foreword by
The Rev Canon Dr Johannes Arens
Canon Precentor, Leicester Cathedral

Winchester, UK
Washington, USA

First published by Chronos Books, 2016
Chronos Books is an imprint of John Hunt Publishing Ltd., Laurel House, Station Approach,
Alresford, Hants, SO24 9JH, UK
office1@jhpbooks.net
www.johnhuntpublishing.com

For distributor details and how to order please visit the 'Ordering' section on our website.

Text copyright: Canon David Jennings 2015

ISBN: 978 1 78535 430 4
Library of Congress Control Number: 2016931757

A CIP catalogue record for this book is available from the British Library.

Design: Lee Nash

Printed and bound in the USA by Edwards Brothers Malloy

We operate a distinctive and ethical publishing philosophy in all
areas of our business, from our global network of authors to
production and worldwide distribution.

CONTENTS

IN MEMORIAM

This book is dedicated to the memory of
The Rev Geoffrey Cuming,
who taught me liturgy at Kings' College, London,
and Father Kenneth Leech,
who was an inspiration for my ministry.

Acknowledgments

I am grateful for the teaching I received at Kings' College, London, and especially that from the late Rev Geoffrey Cuming, who guided me through my special subject on the University of London's Bachelor of Divinity course, sixteenth and seventeenth century English and Scottish liturgy.

At St Augustine's College, Canterbury, the late Father Ken Leech, the chaplain, opened my eyes to the social and political witness of the Christian faith, but rooted in the daily offices and Eucharistic worship of the Church.

Bishop David Silk, a former Archdeacon of Leicester and a member of the Church of England's Liturgical Commission, often gave me good and sound advice.

The Parish Church of the Assumption of Our Lady, Hinckley, and the vicar, the late Rev E W Platt, later Canon, instilled in me an appreciation of the Book of Common Prayer which, although critical in many respects, has never been lost.

The Parish Church of St Catherine, Burbage, whilst Rector for 27 years, enabled me to develop and even experiment with liturgical forms and developments within the Church of England, and for which I shall always be grateful.

Finally, my wife Anne, my most severe critic, has challenged me to write something more populist than a book on liturgy, but nevertheless has supported me in engaging with an area which she feels has little contemporary relevance. Although I disagree, I love her for her continued challenge, and much else.

Foreword

The journey from the Prayer Book 1549 to that of 1552 highlights theological issues played out in liturgical texts and actions which still occupy discussion and controversy several hundred years later.

The historic attempt to keep contradictory views and understandings united in one ecclesial national community has made the Church of England unique in being a community bridging catholic and reformed identities. The times of violent clashes about these issues are over in these islands, but to live in a mixed economy of strongly differing views continues to be difficult for the present Church of England – its more current controversies about human sexuality and gender are in their theological width not very different from the controversies in Eucharistic theology of the 16th century.

Although the Church of England of today seems to be changing rapidly, it is interesting to see that this has been the case in different periods of its history, both before and after the Reformation. It still tries to hold together in painful comprehensiveness different and contradictory convictions, and the history of the two Prayer Books, David Jennings tells us in this book, serves as a comforting reminder that extreme and exclusive developments become modified and put into perspective over time – even if it may take quite a long time to do so.

David Jennings' book is a fascinating and encouraging story of ecumenism, making one aware that the Anglican experiment of building a fallible and inclusive church for as many different people as possible has worked for centuries, and continues to be a faithful way of following the command of Our Lord that 'all shall be one'.

The Rev Canon Dr Johannes Arens
Canon Precentor, Leicester Cathedral
December, 2015

Preface

It was 19th May, 1962. I was only 14, but I remember it well. The vicar of my parish church, St Mary's, Hinckley (although one of eight pre-reformation churches dedicated to the Assumption of Our Lady), the Rev E W Platt, hosted a service to celebrate the tercentenary of the 1662 Book of Common Prayer. Invited to the service were the Rev Gordon Baker and his congregation from the Congregational Church in the centre of Hinckley. It was only later that I came to appreciate that it was such ecclesiastical groups and ministers that were unable to subscribe to the 1662 Act of Uniformity, signed on 19th May in that year, which authorised and required the usage of a slightly revised Prayer Book, based upon the 1604 version, which itself was in effect that of 1559, and which resulted in what became known as the Great Ejection. The Act prescribed that any minister who refused to conform to the Prayer Book by St Bartholomew's Day should be ejected. It is estimated that between 2,000 and 2,500 ministers were ejected from their livings. One of these was the vicar of Hinckley, the Rev Thomas Leadbeater. Protestant divines had been invited to the Savoy Conference of 1661, comprising of Episcopalians, representing the suspended Church of England, during the Commonwealth period under the protectorate of the puritan Oliver Cromwell, and the Presbyterians, led by the vicar of Kidderminster, the Rev Richard Baxter, and which was supposed to secure some accommodation between significantly differing ecclesiologies, within a re-established Church of England, with bishops and ceremonies that had proved somewhat contentious since the Reformation of the early sixteenth century.

The conference had broken up with little agreement and continued significant disagreement about what a future Church of England might look like and what its practices might be. It was clear that the Prayer Book of 1662 was not a satisfactory liturgy for a protestant and reformed church as perceived and advocated by Puritans and Presbyterians. This book refers to an earlier period of Prayer Book history, and suggests that the liturgical provision for the Church of England has always been a matter of contention and dispute. The introduction of a vernacular liturgy in 1549, with slightly reformed leanings was resented, even if some of the nuances of reformed doctrine were not immediately observed, especially in the south-western corner of England where English was as little understood as Latin. Further and more draconian changes as represented by the 1552 Book perhaps contributed to the positive acceptance of a return to the Latin Mass when Mary I came to the throne in 1553, following the death of her young half-brother, Edward VI. Persecution and public burnings created an attitude of relief at the accession of Elizabeth I in 1558, and a reception of a revised Prayer Book in 1559. The 1604 Book, enacted with the accession of James I, was without controversy. However, the attempt by William Laud, Archbishop of Canterbury in the reign of Charles I, to impose a form of the more Catholic Prayer Book of 1549 on the Scottish Church in 1637, gave rise in part to the Civil War, the executions of both Laud and Charles, and a Presbyterian order for the Church of Scotland, which exists to this day. Although Prayer Book controversies were dormant for the next 250 years, dispute and argument was to erupt again with the proposed revisions of the late 1920s. It was not until the introduction of alternative orders and books in the latter years of the twentieth century that liturgical reforms adopted a more peaceful and accommodating form, although not without significant disagreement especially concerning the Eucharist, contemporary forms of words and Eucharistic prayers. However, even throughout recent changes and usages, the Church of England has ensured that the 1662 version of the Prayer Book is the standard and normative liturgical text within which the doctrine of the Church is still to be found and located.

It is beyond the scope of this small book to detail the history of the Prayer Book to the present day. Others have dealt with this in a much more comprehensive way. However, it is my contention that the seeds of liturgical divisions and disputes can be located in just three years, between the two Prayer Books of 1549 and 1552. The controversies and arguments surrounding both the reforms of words and church ornaments and adornments continue to this day, although with perhaps less heat and aggression. This is not to suggest that the issues surrounding reform are not still deeply held, it is just that we live in more tolerant and polite times. The question remains not only that of the validity and necessity of the changes between 1549 and 1552, but also who was mainly responsible for the radical departures represented by the two books, and on what theological and ecclesiological bases such were implemented. For the purpose of conciseness, I shall focus upon the Eucharistic liturgies. Again, others have examined other services within the respective books.

In 1962, the aforementioned vicar of Hinckley erected notice boards at every entrance to St Mary's Church, which were the main path routes to the local park, used extensively by courting couples; notices which detailed 1662 to 1962 with thanks to God for the Book of Common Prayer. It would have been difficult, if not impossible, to gage the impact of the notice to those passing through for whatever purpose. However, Prayer Book controversy and subsequent impact has been a feature of Church of England life since 1549, and throughout subsequent arguments and revisions.

David Jennings
November, 2015

Introduction

It is accepted knowledge that Henry VIII, having initiated the break of the Church in England from the authority of the Church in Rome and the Pope, was not interested in a protestant reformation, for what became the Church of England. However, many of his ministers, both secular and religious, including chief minister, Thomas Cromwell, before his downfall, were more interested in a reformation, and sought to push the king in a more protestant and evangelical direction. The resoluteness, power and authority of Henry made such moves difficult, risky and problematic. There were moments, however, when the king leaned in a reformed direction, but such were short lived and he would quickly revert to his natural catholic instincts. Henry always valued his title of Defender of the Faith, given to him by Pope Leo X, on 11th October, 1521, for his refutation of Lutheran doctrine and theology contained in his pamphlet, *Assertio septem sacramentorum adversus Martinum Lutherum* ('Declaration of the seven sacraments against Martin Luther'). When Henry broke with the papacy, Pope Paul III deprived him of this title, but it was restored by parliament in 1544. The title still adorns the coinage of contemporary British monarchs from the time of George I, in the form of Fid. Def. or F.D. In the Act forbidding Papal Dispensations and Payment of Peter's Pence, 1534 (25 Hen. VIII, c.21.), Henry's doctrinal position is stated clearly as there being no intention to 'vary from the congregation of Christ's Church in any things concerning the very articles of the Catholic faith of Christendom'.

For the ordinary person in the pew, although the formal and legal break with Rome occurred between the years 1534 and 1536, such would hardly have made any impact, either positively or negatively. The defining pieces of legislation in particular were The Act of Supremacy, 1534 (26 Hen. VIII, c.1), and The Act

Extinguishing the Authority of the Bishop of Rome, 1536 (28 Hen. VIII, c.10). Other acts of parliament secured the process of ensuring the authority of the king over and above that of the pope, not least in respect of the recognition of the marriage to Anne Boleyn, various financial transactions, and the granting of licences, all of which brought the matter of the governance of the Church firmly into the hands of the king.

However, there would have been little observable or practical difference in the form and conduct of public worship throughout the remainder of Henry's reign. Although the Ten Articles of 1536, adopted by Convocation at the wish of the king and imposed by his sole authority, leaned in a Lutheran direction, more for political expediency than theological conviction, there was little to suggest anything approaching a radical turn in a protestant direction. The lead signature to the Articles was Thomas Cromwell, whom the king had made his vicegerent, thereby investing him with power to execute all the functions which Henry claimed as Supreme Head of the English Church. Cromwell's signature preceded that of Thomas Cranmer, the Archbishop, and those of other prelates and divines. How much Cranmer supported the provision of the articles is not known, and where his own theological and liturgical thinking now lay is a matter for discussion and possible dispute, although it appears that both Cromwell and Cranmer were initially attracted to Lutheranism. However, within a year a document entitled the Institution of a Christian Man, commonly known as the Bishop's Book, was drawn up at the king's command by a large committee of prelates and divines. After much debate, it was completed in July 1537. Unofficially, it replaced the Ten Articles, although not officially authorised, but rather recommended. It reflected a much more catholic and conservative theological position and emphasis. What were the archbishop's views, and did Cranmer have any say or input into the drafting and content? What is clear is Cranmer's opposition to The Act of Six Articles of 1539 (31 Hen.

VIII, c.14) which defined traditional catholic belief, and was opposed not only by the Archbishop, but also Bishop Shaxton of Salisbury and Bishop Latimer of Worcester, the latter two resigning their sees in protest. There was no discernible trajectory of reform which could be identified with a reformation that could be identified with the various protestant streams emerging in continental Europe.

There were, however, during the period prior to the death of Henry VIII in 1547, some minor but significant liturgical changes which were very much instigated by Henry's Archbishop of Canterbury, Thomas Cranmer. These will be detailed in the following chapter, but suffice it to say that although the externals of the catholic faith and practice were observed, the changes indicated a direction towards something that could be described as more protestant. How far such changes might have gone or led, given the historical and personnel issues of the reign of the succeeding king, Henry's only surviving son, the frail Edward VI, is difficult to determine or identify. Even more problematic, for our purposes, is the extent to which Archbishop Cranmer was both responsible for existing and future changes in the theology and liturgy of the English Church, and where did his heart and thinking really reside? Cranmer, clearly, was a pivotal figure on the English ecclesiastical scene, and he was much influenced by the continental Reformation, initially from a Lutheran and German context, and later, possibly, from a Calvinist and Zwinglian Swiss context. This possible change of emphasis on the part of Cranmer is not entirely clear and is subject to further and continued debate. Such will form the substance of this book as the question of Cranmer's involvement in the form and content of the second Prayer Book of 1552 is considered in comparison with and consideration of known changes between the period 1539 with the publication of The Act of Six Articles (31 Hen. VIII, c.14) and 1556, the death of Thomas Cranmer at the stake in Oxford. Were there other influences at work upon the new and very young King Edward VI, and the influence, if not power of his ministers, regents and advisers, possibly over Cranmer himself? The question revolves around what were Cranmer's views and intentions throughout the period. Did these change of his own volition and instigation, and could he be responsible for such significant changes himself within just three years? Who might have been the other players in the process of liturgical conservatism or reform that would have influence upon the dramatic changes that occurred within these three crucial years at the end of Edward's brief reign?

We shall see.

Chapter One

Before 1549

There was a period of two years after the death of Henry VIII in 1547 and the introduction of the 1549 Prayer Book. It was, however, a period of incremental liturgical reform, albeit within the context of the familiar Latin Mass, which Henry had no wish to displace. The most notable feature of the period was the increasing use of English in respect of insertions in the Mass. Three events were particularly important during this period:

i)   The 22nd of Edward VI's Injunctions (1547) required that the epistle and gospel be read at High Mass in English;
ii) In the same year the Act against Revilers and for Receiving in Both Kinds restored the receiving of the cup to the laity;
iii) In March 1548 there was published on royal authority The Order of the Communion.

It should also be noted that the 28th Injunction of Edward VI set forth what was to become one of the central and visible planks of the royal visitation of 1547. In the injunction, clergy and people were to 'take away, utterly extinct and destroy all shrines, covering of shrines, all tables, candlesticks, trindles or rolls of wax, pictures, paintings and all other monuments of feigned miracles, pilgrimages, idolatry, and superstition; so that there remained no memory of the same'. The impact of this upon the ordinary worshipper would have been significant, and possibly disturbing. It was a sign of things to come.

The use of English within the Mass was not as contentious as other incremental reforms. Henry, during the previous reign, had no particular scruples about the use of the vernacular in portions of the liturgy and elsewhere. Apart from certain parts of the country where English was not the first spoken language, the only other concern was whether the increasing use of English presaged more fundamental and protestant reforms and developments. Such, as history proved, was not without foundation. However, in 1546 Henry advanced two steps towards reform: the abolition of certain liturgical ceremonies such as ringing bells all night on All Hallows' evening, kneeling to the rood on Palm Sunday, and the veneration of the cross on Good Friday. The second was 'to change the Mass into a Communion'. Neither reform could be described as drastic, although somewhat significant, but occurring a year before the King's death provided a bench mark and template for subsequent and more radical changes during the reign of the next king. Geoffrey Cuming writes:

> *'Although Henry's policy of enforcing strict Catholic doctrine and practice made official progress towards liturgical reform necessarily slow, unofficial pressure continued to build up, and Cranmer felt that some degree of uniformity should be pursued which would at any rate quieten the advocates of reform for a time'*
> ('A History of Anglican Liturgy')

Did Cranmer's concern for uniformity and the desire to quieten reform reflect his true thinking and position in respect of theological and liturgical change, or was his position purely and solely pragmatic? The potential for upheaval and unrest was always a paramount concern for Tudor England, and Cranmer may merely have been reflecting the concern for order and stability.

The distribution of communion in the two kinds of bread and wine was clearly an innovation, but perhaps not too momentous in that the laity rarely received communion. The priest would receive in both kinds but the laity would content themselves with observing the celebration with personal devotions such as saying the rosary, and would often only receive communion, in one kind, once a year at Easter. The reformers, both in England and on the continent, wished for more regular reception of communion and in both kinds, but such was difficult to enforce given the long tradition of annual communication following confession and absolution. Two kinds were a novelty, but not so much of a novelty on a once a year basis. A major problem, however, and one with a cost element, was the necessity of purchasing larger chalices.

The 1548 *Order of the Communion* was far more significant in that it introduced into the Mass a new order that was clearly and observably of a more protestant and reformed nature. It is possible, given that the outward signs and ceremonies were retained, that many may not have appreciated or understood the theological tradjection that the order represented. Lest, however, that anyone should be in doubt, the order was prefaced by a royal proclamation which promises 'the reformation and setting forth of such godly orders as may be most to God's glory'. The Act of Parliament of December 1547 which enjoined communion in both kinds and the Order which was printed in March 1548, stressed the worthy receiving of communion by the laity and encouraged due preparation, not least given that private confession was no longer compulsory. The general confession in the order addressed this particular issue.

The *Order* begins with an exhortation to be read the previous Sunday. The remainder occurs after the priest's communion, and consisted of the following:

Another exhortation
A warning against impenitent reception
An invitation to confession
A general confession
An absolution

Four sentences of scripture
A prayer for worthy reception
The words of administration
The final blessing

It has been suggested that there are Lutheran influences in the Order and its position in the Mass. However, Cuming argues:

> 'The Order remains firmly within the framework of the Mass, and impenitently sacerdotal in outlook: the confession and the prayer for worthy reception are both to be said by the priest, "or else by one of the ministers, in the name of all them that shall receive the Communion"; the congregation is allowed only to say "Amen" to the blessing.'
>
> ('A History of Anglican Liturgy')

Much of this Order was to appear and remain in subsequent Prayer Books, albeit in a different place and within a liturgy that eventually bore little resemblance to the Mass.

For the ordinary parishioner, including lay officials such as churchwardens, of greater notice was the disposal of church furnishings and ornaments. These affected an observable difference in the conduct and experience of public worship, more perhaps than the use of English in the Mass, and the insertion of additional forms such as *The Order of the Communion*. Some of the removals took the form of destruction, and others by way of sale. Eamon Duffy draws attention to this reality:

> 'The removal of images and in due course altars was required by authority, and, where necessary, enforced. But the apparently voluntary sale of religious objects was almost as striking a feature of the parish records of Edwardine England as was iconoclasm.'
>
> ('The Stripping of the Altars')

Duffy continues to indicate that many of the sold objects were connected with the cult of saints, many associated with the Blessed Sacrament, and much else that reflected a cult of the dead. All focused on a more overtly protestant form of outward observance which was increasingly evidenced in the manner of liturgical celebration and teaching. The years between the death of the 'catholic' King Henry in 1547 and the provision of a 'reformed' prayer book in 1549 witnessed considerable changes, but still within a recognisable form of words and within an understood and familiar Mass.

It was clear that the first two years of Edward's reign were a time of both consolidation, in terms of what had already been achieved in liturgical reform, and a preparation for more significant reforms. There were now significant players on the political stage to press for a form of Protestantism as perceived and experienced in continental Europe. The king himself, although sympathetic, lacked both age and strength to effect the direction of travel. As well as Archbishop Cranmer, now given more reign and scope for long desired changes, a major player on the political scene was Somerset, the Lord Protector of the realm. He was a convinced Protestant with significant power and influence, and uncle to the king. The reforms of the period 1547 to 1549 were promoted by the Archbishop and Protector with keen eyes for further and subsequent liturgical developments, and as represented by the 1549 Prayer Book.

Into this liturgical and ecclesiological mix was the accretion of wealth and power that was consequent upon what came to be seen as the overthrow of Catholicism. David L. Edwards writes of the period:

'It has been estimated that in the course of the reign of Edward VI Crown lands with a capital value (twenty years' rent) exceeding £400,000 were granted away, mostly to members of his council or senior government officials and lands which were to yield much

more than the £320,000 paid for them were sold off by the Crown.'
('Christian England Volume 2: From the Reformation to the 18th Century')

This perhaps questions the integrity and theological commitment of those engaged and involved with the reformation agenda. Edwards continues to suggest that whilst the Catholicism of the Princess Mary was tolerated, the liberating of protestant ideas and propaganda assisted Somerset and his associates in their determination to transform the appearance and activities of the churches; they clearly were determined to destroy the public position of the medieval Church. He asserts:

'Otherwise they could not be sure of retaining the pleasant houses which they were making for themselves out of the Church's ruins.'
('Christian England Volume 2: From the Reformation to the 18th Century')

It is unlikely, however, that Archbishop Cranmer was caught up in this seizure of wealth and power, although the process would not be antithetical to his purposes and desire for reform. However, the question remains concerning the direct influence of the Archbishop on the reforms of the period and his own complicity in driving the reforms. At a number of places within his archiepiscopate, Cranmer has either changed his position or been compliant with others with greater reforming zeal than he might have possessed within his own thinking and volition. Given the variety of influences upon the liturgical and reforming mind of the Archbishop, it is difficult to determine with any certainty where his own mind and inclination lay. Experimentation is a relatively easy endeavour, especially when plagiarising sources currently being explored in Lutheran Germany, or later in Calvinist Geneva. However, a clear direction and outcome for an English reformation is at best imprecise, or at worst confused. Horton Davies suggests that:

> *'In his study and in his mind, however, Archbishop Cranmer was*
> *conducting other liturgical experiments.'*
> ('Worship and Theology in England; From Cranmer to
> Hooker 1534-1603')

Davies states that the experiments were entirely concerned with the simplification of the Daily Office, and following Frere, believes that Cranmer's thinking in this matter could be traced to a period before the accession of Edward VI, and perhaps very shortly afterwards. Again, there is ambiguity concerning Cranmer's thinking and implementation of liturgical change in this period prior to 1549, and subsequent to the production and enforcement of the First Prayer Book in that year. It is my contention that the Archbishop was absorbing and perhaps confused by many influences which continued to create liturgical changes with little consistency of thought and purpose. Such produced the liturgical confusion that bedevilled the English Church throughout the second half of the sixteenth century and through to the middle of the seventeenth with the publication and authority of the 1662 Book of Common Prayer.

Before considering the 1549 book, it might be useful to identify the influences that pressed upon Cranmer. The Lutheran dimension was that provided by the Church Order of Cologne *(Pia Deliberatio)*, which was prepared for Herman von Wied, the Prince-Archbishop, by Martin Bucer. The latter was to continue to exercise influence upon Cranmer beyond the 1549 reforms. This Order had clear impact upon the 1548 *Order of the Communion*. However, the Order itself was based upon the work of Andreas Osiander's Brandenburg-Nuremberg Church Order. Osiander was the uncle of Cranmer's wife, Margaret, which perhaps indicates another level of influence. Furthermore, many important continental divines sought refuge in England from persecution under the Emperor Charles V. Among them were Peter Martyr (December, 1547), Francis Dryander (January, 1548), John a Lasco and Valerand Poullain (September, 1548), and Martin Bucer (April, 1549). Exiles from England also returned, including Miles Coverdale and John Hooper. These were all to impute influence on the English reformation and consequential liturgical reforms, often reflecting the part of Europe from whence they came and the theological emphases thereby reflected and practised. In encouraging this influx, Cranmer in his *Original Letters* indicated his wish *'to have the assistance of learned men who, having compared their opinions together with us, may do away with all doctrinal controversies, and build up an entire system of true doctrine'*. What influences were really at play from such a body of influential reformers upon the mind and practice of Archbishop Cranmer, recognising the political confusions and vagaries of the English Reformation? In respect of Cranmer's stated hope, Cuming suggests:

'Even if this hope was not to be realized, both groups, though too late to have much influence on the impending production of an English Prayer Book, were to make their contribution when the book came to be revised'
('A History of Anglican Liturgy')

We shall see.

Chapter Two

1549 and all that

For many in 1549, it was sincerely held, from the protestant position, that the Prayer Book was but a temporary and interim rite, pending further revision. The reformer, Martin Bucer, who met Cranmer for the first time in April, 1549, firmly believed such to be the case and wrote to his colleagues in Strasburg:

> 'I gather that some concessions have been made both to a respect for antiquity, and to the infirmity of the present age; such as, for instance, the vestments commonly used in the sacrament of the Eucharist, and the use of candles; so also in regard to the commemoration of the dead, and the use of chrism ... They affirm that there is no superstition in these things, and that they are only to be retained for a time, lest the people, not yet thoroughly instructed in Christ, should be too extensive innovations be frightened away from Christ's religion, and that rather they may be won over.'
> ('Original Letters' in 'Epistolae Tigurinae', 1848)

It is this position that turns upon the question as to how far Cranmer, and those who supported him and his liturgical reforms, were committed to the form and theology of the 1549 book. If there was little commitment, the accusation of deceit and duplicity could be legitimately levelled against the archbishop. Given the efforts and drive behind the direction of reform in the first two years of Edward's reign, and the clear political support as represented by Protector Somerset, it is unlikely that the work and input that lay behind the drafting, publication and authorisation of the 1549 book was not considered to be of worth and value. Davies suggests that:

'The publication of the First English Book of Common Prayer generated three responses, varying from acceptance through temporary acquiescence to dissatisfaction'
('Worship and Theology in England: From Cranmer to Hooker 1534-1603')

However, it ought to be noted that the book had the force of law via an Act of Uniformity with heavy fines for noncompliance. Such would encourage, willingly or reluctantly, acceptance. The Spanish protestant scholar, Dryander evidenced a positive estimation of the book when he wrote to Bullinger in Strasburg on 5th June, 1549:

'A book has now been published a month or two back, which the English churches received with great satisfaction.'
('Original Letters Relative to the English Reformation')

For other mainly continental reformers, the book was anything but satisfactory. For example, John Butler wrote to Thomas Blaurer on 16th February, 1550:

'The affairs of religion are now, through the mercy of God, in a more favourable, considering the state of infancy and rudeness of our nation. Baptism, for instance, and the Lord's Supper, are celebrated with sufficient propriety, only that some blemishes in respect to certain ceremonies, such for instance as the splendour of vestments, have not yet been done away with.'
('Original Letters Relative to the English Reformation')

What was Cranmer's position in respect of acceptance of the 1549 book, whether wholehearted or begrudging? Davies suggests, quoting Richard Hilles' letter to Bullinger on 4th June, 1549, that:

'.... Cranmer is more anxious to please the German than the Swiss

divines, and that Bucer, who had recently come to Cambridge, might
keep him conservative.'
('Worship and Theology in England: From Cranmer to
Hooker 1534-1603')

There can be little doubt that the 1549 book was a conservative
revision of the Mass along predominantly Lutheran lines. The
later 1552 book clearly reflected the Swiss reformation of
possibly John Calvin in Geneva, but more likely that of Ulrich
Zwingli in Zurich.

What, therefore, was the structure and form of this conservative revision which was accepted or welcomed with the imprint
of previous changes and developments by Archbishop Thomas
Cranmer? The title for the Eucharist gives an immediate
indication of the direction of travel: 'The Supper of the Lord and
the Holy Communion, commonly called the Mass'. 'The Supper
of the Lord' is the name for the service given by Herman von
Wied, the Prince-Archbishop of Cologne; 'the Mass' is both the
medieval and the Lutheran name; 'the Holy Communion' is a
vernacular name used now for the first time as applicable to the
whole service. How far did the book represent Cranmer's desire
to appease conflicting viewpoints and positions within the
English Church concerning a reformed Church that could both
reflect a protestant position, whilst at the same time enable a
catholic interpretation, if not continued practice with a familiar
Mass? Cuming suggests:

'In the book of 1549 Cranmer was trying to edge a nation notorious for
its conservatism into accepting a reformed service, though, for all its
comprehensiveness, the book turned out to have gone almost too far.'
('A History of Anglican Liturgy')

For the layperson, the textual alterations, amendments and
omissions may not have been that observable, and thereby not

controversial. The outward signs, ceremonies and rituals would have attracted more attention and possible concern if not unrest. For the present purpose, suffice it to note that the form and structure of the 1549 Eucharistic rite differed little from the former and familiar Sarum service. A good example would be the retention of the majority of the Collects with all but eight of the sixty-three simply being translations from the Latin. The discarded Collects were those asking for the prayers of the saints. Also, the Epistles and the Gospels were taken from Sarum with few changes. The only changes to the structure, apart from the already familiar *The Order of the Communion* location before the priest's communion rather than afterwards, concern the opening of the service with the Lord's Prayer and the placing of the sermon before the offertory. The latter reflects Lutheran practice and is indicative of the German influence upon Cranmer and his reforms. Also, a sermon or homily is expected every Sunday as opposed to quarterly. There are other minor prayer additions, including a Collect for the king, various biblical passages, a removal of some chants and a reduction in the number of Proper Prefaces. Whilst such may not have been appreciated or observable, and in themselves would not necessarily indicate a significant change or diversion from catholic theology as reflected in the liturgy, what would have struck the observer in the pew would have been the prohibition of the elevation of the host at the centre of the Canon of the Mass. For many, such was the focus and highlight for congregations who often had little to no understanding of Latin, and would have been unlikely to receive communion. The elevation of the host and chalice was the purpose of attendance at Mass, and represented the worship and adoration of God in Christ upon the altar where the sacrifice of the Mass was offered. It was this latter understanding of the Eucharist that the reformers, including with little doubt Archbishop Cranmer, were so opposed to and who sought to expunge from all reformed liturgies to a greater or lesser degree.

The reduction in a number of ceremonies and the removal of images would have some impact and clearly, for the reformers, represented forms of idolatry, but the retention of much of the Mass, including vestments, would enable a belief that it was still the Mass that was being celebrated, albeit in a slightly different way, with slightly different words, and with a book now published containing all the services of the Church in English. Doubts would have crept in without the elevation.

How much of the 1549 Book was genuinely the work of Thomas Cranmer and how much was an accurate reflection of his own theology? In an essay entitled 'The Tudor Prayer Books', Gordon Jeanes writes:

'The new liturgy was very much the work of one man: Thomas Cranmer. This is not to claim that he composed every word of it......As for Cranmer's purpose, it is clear that the Prayer Book embodied his personal theology. The Archbishop has often been labelled as influenced by one Reformer or another, but the truth is that he was his own man and the Prayer Book was his book.'
('Comfortable Words: Polity, Piety and The Book of Common Prayer')

Even during the reign of Henry VIII when the pragmatist Cranmer flowed with the theological tide of the Supreme Head of the Church of England, he was able to exert some influence towards a more reformed stance. However, this was very much of a conservative nature, and at the time more reflective of Lutheran theology, with liturgical implications. His early support and acceptance of the essential Lutheran emphasis on justification by faith alone would be given credence within his thinking and reforms. Such could have been supported by his wife's Lutheran uncle, Andreas Osiander, and Philip Melanchthon. Given the time that Cranmer had to consider what a reformed English liturgy might look like, and what reasons he might offer to the English people for a reformation which more than likely would not be popular, it would be natural, after the death of Henry and the ascent to the throne of the boy King Edward VI, and mindful of the conservative protestant views of Protector Somerset, that a catholic looking liturgy with protestant leanings and emphases would be the first fruits of his liturgical foray. In an essay entitled 'Thomas Cranmer', Patrick Collinson suggests:

> 'In 1549 Cranmer was constrained: constrained by the need to carry with him his Episcopal and other clerical colleagues; constrained politically by the theologically moderate regime of Somerset; constrained by the objection to putting into people's mouths sentiments which were not yet wholly theirs; and, moreover, constrained to an extent which cannot now be exactly measured by his own veneration for traditional structures and language, a conservative liturgical instinct in tension with the reformist thrust of his theology.'
> ('The English Religious Tradition and the Genius of Anglicanism')

The conundrum of where Cranmer's heart and treasure reside continues to fascinate and perplex, especially given it was to emerge but three years later. The constraints that Collinson identifies lead him to conclude:

> 'This last difficulty has led some authorities to the opinion that 1549 was Cranmer's preferred liturgy, because closer to traditional forms; others to insist that 1552 was a plainer, truer expression of what he intended.'
> ('The English Religious Tradition and the Genius of Anglicanism')

Collinson, however, is more explicit when he infers that:

'...in our own age learned scholars have been misled into believing what is most unlikely: that Cranmer changed his doctrine of the eucharist (which is to say, his religion) between 1549 and 1552.'
('The English Religious Tradition and the Genius of Anglicanism')

We shall see.

Chapter Three

1552 revolution

Whilst the externals and many of the words of the 1549 Prayer Book would be familiar to all but the theologically and liturgically illiterate, there could be no mistake about the difference reflected in the 1552 Book. With regard to the 1549 book, Cuming writes:

> *'Many priests used the book, but disguised it in all the external trappings and gestures of the Mass, converting the popular 'Lady Mass' into a 'Communion of Our Lady.'*
> ('A History of Anglican Liturgy')

Although most of the interiors of parish churches were being changed by the removal of images, paintings and some ornaments, which had been taking place in the period between 1549 and 1552, the new book specifically required the removal of altars to be replaced by a simple communion table set in the chancel on an east/west axis as opposed to a position against the east wall on a north/south axis, with significantly different words for the liturgy, including the relocation of some familiar words and texts, together with a noticeable change in the vesture of the presiding minister. Kenneth Stevenson, in referring to the changes in the 1552 Book, compared to that of 1549, points out that:

> *'...and when we look at 1552, the process is taken still further. Apart from the abolition of vestments, except the surplice, the altar is now described as the table, and it is set alongside the people in the chancel to avoid any sacrificial symbolism connected with traditional orientation.'*
> ('Eucharist and Offering')

Returning exiled refugee divines, who had experienced more reformed liturgies, whilst appreciating the reformation reflected in the 1549 book, nevertheless looked forward to further liturgical changes in a more reformed direction. Cuming suggests:

> 'they were prepared to tolerate the retention of ceremonies only as a temporary expedient. Even this was unacceptable to John Hooper, the leading English disciple of Zwingli, who pronounced the book 'very defective, and of doubtful construction, and, in some respects indeed, manifestly impious'.'

('A History of Anglican Liturgy')

There could be no doubting that the 1552 Prayer Book was a reformed liturgy, which tended to have more in common with the reforms of Ulrich Zwingli in Zurich rather than those of John Calvin in Geneva, and most certainly a departure from those of Martin Luther in Germany.

The politics of the day had an impact upon both the 1549 and the 1552 books, which suggests external influences upon future liturgical changes in addition, if not in place of, ecclesiastical desires and motivations. In what respects, therefore, did the 1552 Book differ from that of 1549 and how does such reflect a different theological position concerning the nature, understanding and experience of the Eucharist? Apart from clearly visible external changes, the words of the liturgy were not so much changed as relocated. There were some noticeable omissions, but the major alteration and upon which much of the understanding of the Book's underlying interpretation was based, centred upon the words used at the distribution of communion. In place of 'The Body/Blood of our Lord Jesus Christ which was given/shed for thee, preserve thy body and soul unto everlasting life', the following words were inserted: 'Take and eat/drink this in remembrance that Christ died/Christ's Blood was shed for thee/and feed on him in thy heart by faith with thanksgiving/and be thankful'. There could be no clearer statement and indication that the presence of Christ was located in the heart of the believer and recipient, rather than in the elements of bread and wine, albeit recently consecrated, although the latter term was not used of the preceding prayer containing the words of institution. Furthermore, there were to be no prescribed manual acts on the part of the priest in respect of, or more specifically over the elements at the reciting of the dominical words of institution. At what is called the offertory, there is no specific instruction to even place the bread and wine to be used for communion upon the altar/table. The service could proceed without the elements being at hand, and even after the service it is suggested that any bread or wine left could be taken away by the curate for his own use. Some would suggest that the 1552 Communion Service reflects an absence as opposed to a presence. The clear emphasis is upon the individual receiving the elements by faith, and not something that is somehow present within the elements themselves.

The order and structure of the 'revised' service would have been noticeable, although many might not have appreciated the significance. R T Beckwith in his essay 'The Anglican Eucharist: From Reformation to Restoration' observes:

'In 1552 the structure and content of the service were changed much more strikingly than in 1549. The introit psalm and the offertory of the elements were omitted, the Decalogue was introduced, the Gloria in Excelsis was moved from the ante-communion to the post-communion, and the devotional material from the 1548 Order of the Communion was once again shifted.'
('The Study of Liturgy')

Stevenson points out that the focus and locus of the communion rite is now the people and not the elements. He writes that:

'The people are at the heart of the drama, so that having made their offering of money and having offered solemn intercession, they are exhorted and confess. They give thanks and pray humbly about communion. The bread and wine are set apart in a carefully worded manner, again placing emphasis on the people ("that we," contrasted with the 1549 epiclesis). The elements are immediately consumed, after which the people either give thanks for communion.... or they pray for the acceptance of the sacrifice of themselves... 1552... aggressively points to the communicants as the Church, to be prepared for eating and drinking, but at the expense of any objective activity.'

('Eucharist and Offering')

The fragmentation of what still would have been called a canon in the Mass in 1549 was an indication that the 1552 Book represented a radical departure from anything that could imply that the rite was a propitiatory sacrifice, offered for the living and the departed. The author, or perhaps rather editor of the service, clearly wished to remove any suggestion of transubstantiation, whereby the elements of bread and wine quite literally became the actual body and blood of Christ through the words and actions of the priest. The Prayer for the Church which introduced the canon in 1549 was separated from what was the consecration and oblation, with the exhortations following. Those parts of the 1548 Order for Communion which comprised the invitation to confession, the confession, the absolution and the comfortable words then followed, rather than immediately preceding the administration of communion, as in 1549. The sursum corda followed with the Prayer of Humble Access located between that and the consecration. What was the final part of the canon, namely the Prayer of Oblation, was now located after communion and the Lord's Prayer, and as an alternative to the Prayer of Thanksgiving. It was clear that this re-ordering, and some word adjustment to conform to a more reformed position, indicated that the focus of the service was worthy reception of communion taking place immediately after the consecration, and was deemed, thereby, to be a continuation of the dominical words of institution, reflecting the receptionist position that the benefits received were appropriated in the heart and belief of the communicant, and not by virtue of any ontological change in the elements or by virtue of a priest's offering of a sacrifice. Cuming writes of this:

> 'The changes in language were nearly all dictated by doctrinal controversy. The Prayer for the Church was not only moved, but, as both Bucer and Hooper wished, shorn of any reference to the saints or the departed; it is now only for the "Church militant herein earth". A whole series of changes were aimed at removing any suspicion of transubstantiation.'
> ('A History of Anglican Liturgy')

The contrast between both the words and the performance of the 1552 Book compared to that of 1549 could not have been more observable and significant. Quite simply, whereas the rite of 1549 could still be described as catholic, that of 1552 was most definitely protestant. There were many influences in the transition within what was a relatively short period of time, politically and ecclesiologically. The fall of the Protector, Somerset, in the autumn of 1549 gave rise to a rumour that the 1549 Book would be withdrawn. However, he was succeeded by Northumberland, who was of a more protestant disposition, and in many respects encouraged the 1552 reformed revision of the rite. Furthermore, the older and more conservative bishops were replaced by men of more evangelical leanings. Conservative bishops, Gardiner and Bonner, had been imprisoned, Rugg resigned, Heath and Day were deprived. Whilst Cranmer and Ridley were in favour of reform, the clear leader and contender for a radical reformation and liturgical reform was John Hooper, who was to become Bishop of Gloucester. He preached before the king in Lent 1550, criticising the 1549 Prayer Book services, including the oaths and vestments required in the Ordination Services. Hooper was encouraged by fellow Zwinglians, Henry Bullinger and John a Lasco, and was imprisoned for refusing to wear vestments for his ordination. His influence on the 1552 Book would be significant, not least given his distain and disgust at the earlier book. Chris Skidmore records of Hooper:

> '"I am so much offended with that book," wrote the reformer John Hooper, "that if it be not corrected, I neither can nor will communicate with the church in the administration of the supper".'
> ('Edward VI: The Lost King of England')

The influence of Martin Bucer through his critique of the 1549 Book and Hooper's hyper and emotional ripostes against the said Book, and given Swiss reformation principles, were going to impact upon any subsequent revision. The conservative Bishop Stephen Gardiner's support for 1549 would have a reverse influence which would presage the desire for further reform. But where were Cranmer's thoughts within this maelstrom of reformation fervour?

For many, both the 1549 and 1552 rites represented not only the work of the Archbishop, Thomas Cranmer, but have also been identified as his legacy to the Church of England. Can this be true?

We shall see.

Chapter Four

Was it Cranmer?

The general and prevailing liturgical assumption is that Thomas Cranmer, Archbishop of Canterbury, was the author and driver of both the 1549 and 1552 Prayer Books. Much of this was rooted and based upon the fact that he had been Henry VIII's archbishop and helped lead the king through the break with Rome and a modicum of reformed leanings, but not always with success. The production of the 1548 Order for Communion was more than likely a Cranmerian production and paved the way for an English and slightly reformed rite in 1549.

Dominic Aidan Bellenger and Stella Fletcher speculate:

'In contrast to his predecessors, Archbishop Thomas Cranmer's reputation has been determined less by physical remains than literary ones, chief among them the Book of Common Prayer (1549 and 1552), though, apart from the collects, it is impossible to be sure about precisely how much of it he personally composed.'
('The Mitre & the Crown: A History of the Archbishops of Canterbury')

What was going on in Cranmer's mind in the three years between 1549 and 1552, and how active was he in the evolution and production of the second Prayer Book of 1552? Relevant to this question is that of how much and how far did the 1549 Book reflect Cranmer's theology? If it was a true reflection, not least given the time he would have considered the rite between the death of Henry in 1547, previous reformed inclinations, and the advent of the 1549 Book, is it possible that his whole theological, ecclesiological and liturgical outlook was so dramatically changed in what might appear a relatively short period of time?

However, those who might adhere to the view that 1552 was the 'real' Cranmer, would have to assert and affirm that 1549 was a cover, or even a deception, whilst his real intentions had been developing for the period prior to 1549. This would leave the question concerning Cranmer's integrity in the authorisation, implementation and use of the 1549 rites as a matter of legitimate conjecture. There is also the political question as to why Cranmer imposed and supported the introduction and compulsory use of a rite which he knew would be both controversial and disturbing if such was not his real and definitive intention? If the consensus is that Cranmer was not responsible, either directly or indirectly, for 1552, then who was or were the instigators and author(s) of the second Book?

Much would revolve and focus upon Cranmer's view of the divine presence in the elements of the Eucharist as it is the point at which 1552 differs significantly with that of 1549. Cranmer's views would seem to have changed over the years subsequent to 1530, but did they evolve from a traditional catholic under-standing to that more in keeping and a reflection of a Lutheran interpretation, or did they continue on a trajectory to a thorough-going Zwinglian and receptionist position? At the proceedings held against Bishop Edmund Bonner of London, by Cranmer and others for initially not using the 1549 Book, and then using it 'discreetly and sadly' in such a way in St Paul's Cathedral with much traditional splendour that it would seem to subvert the rite, Bonner, at the third session, taunted Cranmer's Eucharistic positions. Diarmaid MacCulloch points out:

> '.... he gleefully exploited the contradiction in Eucharistic teaching between the first and the revised editions of the 1548 catechism: "My Lord of Canterbury, I have here a note out of your books that you made touching the blessed sacrament, wherein you do affirm the verity of the body and blood of Christ to be in the sacrament, and I have another book also of yours of the contrary opinion;

which is a marvellous matter".'
('Thomas Cranmer')

That Cranmer possessed the art if not of deception but of concealment, and such not just to do with the fact that he had a wife, cannot be in doubt. The years from 1530 to the end of the reign of Edward VI in 1553 were turbulent, to say the least. Even the theological position of Henry VIII varied, especially during the latter years of his reign. If one wanted to keep one's head, and quite literally, it was necessary to fluctuate in accordance to the variances and vagaries of the monarch, now Supreme Head of the Church of England. Cranmer lived and held the most senior ecclesiastical position during this confused and contested period. He could only do this and survive if he was to be able to tune his thinking and practice to be that of the king he professed to serve, and to whom he bore true allegiance and dependence. It would be surprising, therefore, not to be aware of the deeper thoughts, positions and wishes of the archbishop recognising that subterfuge was a practical survival mechanism. A further question could be whether Cranmer possessed any definable theological, ecclesiological or liturgical thinking, or was he merely a loyal agent and puppet to his master? Rowan Williams suggests that:

'The Communion Orders of 1549, 1552 and 1662 were, of course, political documents in a very strong sense, enforced by Act of Parliament for use in every place of worship in the realm; their authority was coextensive with that of the English Crown. They were not authorized by a Church visibly distinct from the realm, with a different set of laws and distinct class of official interpreters of those laws. Hence, what is enacted in the laws enforcing the use of the Prayer Books is law for both Church and State; for the Church as well as the commonwealth of Christian people living under the rule of the English Crown.'
('Imagining the Kingdom' in 'The Identity of Anglican Worship')

There can be little doubt that Cranmer was a loyal servant of the Crown and supporter of the various pieces of legislation that both created the English Reformation and subsequent liturgies for the emerging Church of England. He was an obedient servant to both Henry VIII and Edward VI and believed strongly in the role of the monarch *vis a vis* the headship of a reformed Church of England, and the right of the Crown to determine the direction of the Church, including its furnishings and the conduct of its worship. It would be surprising if the Archbishop did not advise his king in respect of theological and liturgical matters. However, it is also clear that both Henry and Edward were literate in such matters, and would have no compunction in giving directions to their archbishop or any other bishop. Skidmore writes:

> 'Though Edward may not have put his hand to the 1552 Prayer Book, he continued to maintain a strong interest in the reformed faith and its application. In one celebrated story, Edward sent for Bishop Nicholas Ridley after he had heard his sermon exhorting the rich to charity.... commended Ridley on his sermon but wanted to know how he could do more....'

('Edward V1: The Lost King of England')

In these somewhat volatile and turbulent times, with many influences upon the direction of the reformation in England, would Archbishop Thomas Cranmer, within a relatively short period of time, have radically re-written the Prayer Book he had introduced and enforced upon the English people without direction being given by others, including those who held the highest positions in the land?

I think not.

We shall see.

Chapter Five

Who dunnit?

If not Cranmer, then who could have been responsible for the significant changes that took place in just three years between the 1549 and 1552 Prayer Books? It has already been suggested that the changes in respect of the words of the liturgy were not that significant, although there were clear evidences of a more protestant and reformed direction. However, the most observable deviations were those of order and structure, which in themselves were specifically designed to reflect reformation theology, ecclesiology and liturgy.

Whilst it is suggested that the responsibility for the 1552 Book was unlikely to have been entirely that of Thomas Cranmer, given his significant and central responsibility for the 1549 Book, only three years previous, and his advocacy of the same, as Archbishop of Canterbury he cannot have been both mindful of the changes and what they represented, together with some acceptance of the underlying theology. However, it also needs to be noted that Cranmer was very much the pragmatist. He could also be described as a fair-weather man, and perhaps had a concern to ensure and maintain his not insignificant position as the *de facto* leader of the young reformed Church of England. This might not have been an egocentric position, but perhaps one that sought to protect the Church from other influences represented by the more extreme protestant and catholic advocates.

In the first instance, and given the undeniable Zwinglian thrust and direction of what is known as the Second Edwardine Prayer Book, the first place to look for influence is to John Hooper. It is reputed that Hooper originally entered a Cistercian monastery, but upon the dissolution of religious houses he began to interest himself in the Continental Reformation. He was exiled for heresy and spent much time travelling Europe and settling in Zurich. Hooper returned to England in 1549 and became chaplain to Protector Somerset, providing him with a significant influence at Court. However, it is to be noted that Hooper was perhaps the more articulate and extravagant voice among the returning continental exiles from the reign of Henry VIII, and who had come under the influence not only of Ulrich Zwingli in Zurich, but also of other protestant reformers in that city, and in Geneva. Hooper had already expressed his disgust to various continental friends with the whole of the 1549 Book, and he was not one to resist intemperate language. It was Cranmer who gave Hooper the platform for his radical views by granting him an invitation in 1550 to preach a Lenten course of sermons at Court. Hooper took this opportunity. He took as his theme the book of Jonah, a suitable peg for diatribes against a wicked city. In the third sermon he attacked the continued mention of the saints in the oath of supremacy and the use of vestments required in the Ordinal, since they were 'rather the habit and vesture of Aaron and the gentiles, than of the ministers of Christ'. Cuming states that he:

> '...used the opportunity to deliver some trenchant criticisms of the Prayer Book services, more especially of the oaths and vestments required in the Ordination Services, which had appeared only a day or two before the sermon in question was delivered.'
>
> ('A History of Anglican Liturgy')

Whilst the oath was changed by the king's own hand, Cranmer, supported by Ridley, Bucer and Peter Martyr, upheld the requirement for the appropriate vesture for a bishop at his consecration, and Hooper found himself in prison for his obstinacy in this matter. His capitulation was effected on the basis that he would not have to wear the vestments in his diocese of Gloucester. What is perhaps of interest is that even in 1550,

Cranmer appeared unwilling to alter or amend significant parts of the 1549 liturgy, as represented by the Ordinal. Hooper, on the other hand, clearly wanted to press the reformed principles he had learned and experienced in Zurich. After this skirmish with Cranmer and ecclesiastical authority, would Hooper, and fellow Zwinglian travellers, achieve sufficient influence to press for a wider ranging reform of the Prayer Book that the compliant Cranmer might feel obliged to go along with?

It is perhaps important to note, however, that there were reforms in ceremony and ornaments during the period 1549 to 1552. For example, Bishop Ridley, translated to the bishopric of London in April, 1550, issues a set of Injunctions forbidding, among other things, a detailed list of gestures intended to 'counterfeit the popish Mass, such as 'kiss the Lord's Table......showing the sacrament openly before distribution of the Communion'. Ridley instructed other changes which included the replacement of the high altars in churches with a table. However, such were prohibited whilst yet within the context of the 1549 liturgy with its moderate reformed emphasis, and they do not represent a 'root and branch' reform as was to come in 1552. Davies writes:

'To compound the rubrical problems, it was well known that conservative priests had continued to offer what was in effect an English Mass by retaining the old ceremonial, including many signs and gestures not comprehensively excluded by the rubrics of 1549. Cumulatively these considerations built up a head of reforming pressure which was finally released in 1552.'
('Worship and Theology in England: From Cranmer to Hooker 1534-1603')

The other influence and perhaps pressure for further reform subsequent to 1549 over and above what might have been the wishes of the Archbishop of Canterbury was to be evidenced in the political realm as opposed to that of the ecclesiastic and reformed agenda. Because of his youth, the king, Edward VI, was subject to the regency of the Lord Protector, the Duke of Somerset, his maternal uncle. Somerset, Edward Seymour, Earl of Hertford and Duke of Somerset became Protector of the Realm upon the death of Henry VIII in 1547, having been granted unprecedented powers through which to exercise his authority. He was reported to have been both a reformer and liberal in his social attitudes. His reformation position and principles have been the subject of much debate. Skidmore suggests that in his patronage of a number of protestant ministers, including John Hooper, he:

'.... was something more than a mere moderate in reform....'
('Edward V1: The Lost King of England')

However, Somerset clearly gave support to the committee of the archbishop and certain of the most senior bishops and theologians that met at Chertsey Abbey in September, 1548, and which was responsible for the 1549 Prayer Book. There were divisions of opinions and views in the committee, but after three weeks the new book was delivered to the king at Windsor. Was the resultant 1549 Book therefore representative of Somerset's views, or would he have pressed Cranmer for further reform?

This is something that is unknown in respect of the 1552 Book as Somerset was deposed as Lord Protector in 1549, and ceased to exercise further influence over his nephew, the king, and thereby Cranmer also. His status, if not title, was taken by the eager John Dudley. Although the son of a traitor, Dudley had successfully pushed himself to positions in Henry's court. He had grown dissatisfied with Somerset's leadership and he was closely involved in the coup of October, 1549, which brought about Somerset's downfall. Dudley had been made Earl of Warwick in 1547 and after 1549 was the *de facto* regent to Edward V1. Skidmore describes him as:

'A political chameleon, (who) finally sided with the reformers and Protestants once he realized where Edward's true feelings lay. Having managed to gain control of the Privy Chamber, (he) became President of the Council.'
('Edward V1: The Lost King of England')

Warwick, who became Duke of Northumberland in October, 1551, had considerable power over the king and his careful manipulation of Edward allowed the king to believe that he, Edward, was increasingly grasping the reins of power. Northumberland was a manipulator with strong protestant leanings. In his role of President of the Council, he promoted extreme protestants, including John Hooper. His relationship with Cranmer was often difficult, not least because he opposed the archbishop's reform of canon law. The relationship with Cranmer was further strained by his association and involvement with the militant and vociferous Scottish reformer, John Knox. Northumberland nominated Knox for the bishopric of Rochester and hoped that he would 'be a whetstone to quicken and sharp the Bishop of Canterbury, where he hath need'. Knox refused the appointment, for which Northumberland felt him to be ungrateful. Both Knox and Northumberland had developed strong connections with and approval of the Swiss reformation, and together with their protégé, Hooper, would exert considerable influence in the political life of the nation. Their relationship with the king gave further opportunity to exert Swiss reformation principles. Cranmer would have been both isolated, but also concerned, given his fundamental belief in and support of the royal supremacy, to accede to the young king's wishes. Northumberland took a very keen interest and involvement in the king's education. This would inevitably include theological and liturgical matters. Cranmer would have been the recipient of the intelligent young king's views and would more than likely refrained from direct challenge, and inclined to reflect the same in his progress of the English Reformation. There was an ironic similarity between Northumberland and Cranmer in that both, when under pressure from the Marian catholic resurgence, renounced their protestant inclinations. Cranmer, however, subsequent to his 'trial' in St Mary the Virgin's Church, Oxford, when it was clear that he was to be burnt at the stake, further recanted his recantation. This could be an indication both of Cranmer's volatility when under pressure, but also his personal ambiguity as to his position in respect of the Reformation direction, of which he had been such an integral part since the reign of Henry VIII. Can his stated position, at any one time, and his predilection to be influenced by others, including the much influenced Edward VI, ever be regarded as consistent, let alone trusted? Such may be indicative of an apparent but significant change of position and theological outlook between 1549 and 1552, resulting in the latter liturgical production.

Two further influences could have been brought to bear upon what may be the impressionable character of Archbishop Thomas Cranmer. One might be considered positive and the other negative, but both pushing Cranmer into a position of compliance with further reformation directions.

Martin Bucer was originally a member of the Dominican Order. He began to correspond with Luther in 1518 and left the Order in 1521, subsequently becoming one of the first priests to marry in 1522. By 1523 he began to preach Lutheranism, but following his excommunication his views drew closer to those of Zwingli, especially concerning the Eucharist. In spite of his reformed principles and credentials, he sought rapprochement both between the followers of Luther and Zwingli, and also between Catholics and Protestants. He was unsuccessful in both enterprises, and in 1549 he came to England where he was welcomed by both Edward VI and Cranmer. His popularity and notoriety resulted in the royal appointment as Regius Professor of Divinity at Cambridge, which was a significant position of influence in the flux of the English reformation at the time. Cranmer is reputed to have sought his advice on many issues, and Bucer's influence is clear on the Anglican Ordinal of 1550. Davies writes:

> *'Bucer seems to have had the greatest influence on Cranmer ... Bucer's stay in England was a source of great satisfaction to Cranmer.'*
> ('Worship and Theology in England: From Cranmer to Hooker 1534-1603')

Whilst at Cambridge, Bucer studied the 1549 Book and subsequently submitted a detailed and closely argued criticism in a document now known as the *Censura*. Bucer sent a copy to Peter Martyr, Regius Professor at Oxford, which in turn with his own criticisms were sent to Cranmer. The influence of the *Censura* upon the 1552 Book is difficult to quantify. There were already many voices expressing criticisms, not least those of Peter Martyr and John Hooper, firmly in the Zwinglian camp. Cuming indicates the limited outcome on the 1552 Book:

> *'Bucer submitted approximately sixty criticisms, of which certainly twenty-three, perhaps twenty-five, were embodied in the Book, and an equal number simply ignored. At seven points Bucer offers an alternative form of words, but this is never adopted: the point is taken, but dealt with in some other way.'*
> ('A History of Anglican Liturgy')

Cuming goes on to suggest that the influence of the *Censura* can be overestimated. In some respects, it is confusing for although Bucer appears to veer towards the theology of Zwingli concerning the Eucharist, in other ways he supports the 1549 Book, although publishing a significant critique. Bucer speaks appreciatively of the Communion Service, 'so pure and

religiously conformed to the Word of God, especially for the time
at which it was made.' For Cranmer, influenced by Bucer, even
before he came to England, and the reforms he promoted in
Strasburg, the messages must have been confusing. It would
appear that Bucer held the Lutheran position concerning the
spiritual presence of Christ in the Sacrament, whilst at the same
time abjuring the notion that things could be consecrated rather
than people. The response to the *Censura* and Bucer's commendation of the 1549 Communion Service would accord with that of
Cranmer. However, a marker of criticism was laid which would
be developed by others more eager perhaps for a significant
revision than the one Cranmer might have advocated. This
position and mantle would be taken up by John Hooper, John
Dudley and the King himself. Davies notes that the third member
of Cranmer's foreign advisers in England was John a Lasco. Of a
Lasco he suggests that:

> *'It is just possible that his influence may have turned Bucer as well*
> *as Martyr toward a more radically Memorialist doctrine of the*
> *sacrament which found expression in the Second Prayer Book of*
> *1552.'*
>
> ('Worship and Theology in England: From Cranmer to Hooker
> 1534-1603')

Life must have been very confusing for Thomas Cranmer as he
sought to settle the English Reformation and preserve the peace
and unity of both state and church.

On the other side of the debate and influence was that of
Bishop Stephen Gardiner, from 1525 to 1549 Master of Trinity
Hall, Cambridge, and from 1531, Bishop of Winchester. Although
Gardiner was actively involved in the annulment of Queen
Catherine's marriage, and supported the Royal Supremacy, he
was opposed to the protestant reforms associated with Thomas
Cromwell. In this respect, his views were in accord with those of

King Henry, and by the end of his reign Gardiner was regarded as the chief opponent in England of reformation doctrines. He was imprisoned by Edward VI in 1548 and deprived of his bishopric in 1551.

In what sense, therefore, could it be said that Gardiner influenced Cranmer and had an impact upon the liturgical revisions to the 1549 Book that led to those of 1552? At his trial in 1550, Gardiner produced *An Explication and Assertion of the true Catholic Faith*. This was a reply to Cranmer's explanation of the doctrine underlying the 1549 Book in his *Defence of the true and Catholic Doctrine of the Sacrament of the Body and Blood of our Saviour Christ*. Gardiner wrong-footed Cranmer by identifying passages in the 1549 Book which clearly represented catholic doctrine, rather than that of Cranmer, and warmly commended them. The only way Cranmer could respond to both this commendation and covert criticism of his own position was to alter the text at those places where he gave attention. Cuming suggests:

> 'The effect of Gardiner's criticisms was to make the next revision more narrowly Reformed in doctrine, and harder for a well-disposed Catholic to accept.'
>
> ('A History of Anglican Liturgy')

It would not be unreasonable to suppose that Cranmer came under increased pressure to support a further revision to deny and refute Gardiner's analysis, and there were many surrounding the Archbishop who would be only too willing to take up this mantle and to press ahead with the reform of the 1549 Book along the lines as represented by the Zwinglian school. Cranmer may not have been a significant player in this process which was now gaining a head of steam through the determination of the king, the Duke of Northumberland and Bishop John Hooper.

The 'who dunnit?' question does not directly impact upon the facts and liturgical expressions contained in both the 1549 and 1552 Books. For the present purpose the issue is how much the 1552 Book truly represented Cranmer's Eucharistic position, and which if not perfectly accepting the influences of others upon the ever pragmatic Archbishop, whose primary loyalty was to the king and the Royal Supremacy, who and with what pressure did Cranmer succumb to in acceding to, if not allowing or enabling the more radical book, as opposed to the one which clearly bore his mark in the early years post Henry VIII and the reformation of which Cranmer had been the leading exponent. However, neither can it be asserted that Cranmer was a closet Catholic. His position had clearly moved from that given expression during the reign of Henry VIII and more openly in the reign of Edward VI, by which time there was a Reformation steam roller which was sweeping all before it. It is the contention of this book that Cranmer was not a Zwinglian, as exemplified in the 1552 Book, but rather travelled from a catholic understanding of the Eucharistic presence, through a Lutheran perspective, and residing in that represented by the other French reformer, based in Geneva, namely John Calvin. This position, which was supported by Bucer, Bullinger and Martyr, was known as Virtualism rather than Receptionalism.

We shall see.

Chapter Six

Mary, Mary quite contrary

Mary Tudor was proclaimed Queen in London on 19th July, 1553, and in most of the north by 22nd July. It was clear and understood that Catholicism would be restored and there would be an immediate halt to the Protestant Reformation, and any thought or suggestion that there might be any further liturgical changes as had been witnessed and experienced between the years 1549 and 1552.

For many studies concerning the history of the Prayer Books from that of 1549, the reign of Queen Mary, Edward's half-sister, the daughter of Henry VIII and Catherine of Aragon, is viewed as an interlude in the development of the English Reformation and its liturgical expression. With the untimely death of the young Edward in 1553, the slight hiatus represented by the oft desig-nated nine-day Queen Jane, the accession of the avowedly Catholic Mary would present the Archbishop with not only a theological and reformed difficulty, but one also of personal safety given his involvement in the divorce of the Queen's parents, and the support for and crowning of the king's mistress, Anne Boleyn. Cranmer, as one of the architects of the Royal Supremacy, would also have been compromised by the necessity to exercise the same even for a Catholic monarch. Eamon Duffy opines:

'The reign of Mary Tudor has had few friends among historians, and the regime's religious dimension has provided most of the copy for the bad press. Until relatively recently, almost everyone agreed that Mary's church was backward-looking, unimaginative, reactionary, sharing both the Queen's bitter preoccupation with the past and her tragic sterility. Marian Catholicism, it was agreed, was strong on repression, weak on persuasion.'

('Fires of Faith: Catholic England under Mary Tudor')

There could be little doubt that Mary would seek, as soon as practicably possible, a full return to the Catholic faith, obedience to Rome, and the restoration of the Catholic Mass. It was inconceivable that the Prayer Book, whether of the 1549 or 1552 variety would or could survive. The same would be true of the reforming Archbishop of Canterbury, Thomas Cranmer. For the present purpose, however, it is the contention of this book that whatever its theological and liturgical deficiencies, and whether such truly represented the final reformed position of Cranmer, the 1552 Book would achieve both notoriety and enhanced affection through its abolition and substitution by the pre-reformation Mass than might otherwise have been the case. This position and that of protestant affection and conviction was given significant weight and credence through those who were exiled when Mary came to the throne, and the 1552 Prayer became their liturgy of identity and hope. However, the use of the Book within various European centres of reformed religion also created an impetus for further revision as the exiles became exposed to more radical and reformed criticism of their beloved liturgy. For the ordinary person and worshipper, the restoration of the Mass and the adornment of their parish churches with altars, images, paintings and vestments did not evoke a rebellion, but rather a quiet and perhaps welcome acceptance of that which was familiar and stable. Not least within this process would be the restoration of prayers for departed loved ones, and the promise of heaven through the performance of good works. Gordon Jeanes notes that:

> '*The 1552 Prayer Book enjoyed a life of less than a year. With Edward's death in July 1553 the reversal of religious policy under Mary was taken for granted and many churches did not even wait for government permission before reverting to the "old religion".'*
> ('The Tudor Prayer Books' in 'Comfortable Words: Polity, Piety and the Book of Common Prayer')

The perspective of the Marian changes cannot be appreciated solely through the eyes, teaching and experience of the exiles, as often happens. Duffy notes, concerning the Marian visitation returns:

> 'There is, moreover, considerable evidence that the religious programme of the Marian church was widely accepted, and was establishing itself in the parishes.... the returns also reveal the startling extent to which the depredations of the Edwardine regime had already been repaired, and the herculean efforts being made by clergy, wardens, and parishioners to reconstruct the ritual and sacramental framework of traditional religion.'

('The Stripping of the Altars')

Given the legal underpinning of the Reformation in England, there could not be an instant reversal of all that occurred between the first murmurings of reformation in the reign of Henry VIII, not least through the political and legal aptitude of Chancellor Thomas Cromwell, through to the full blown and continental principles as represented in the 1552 Prayer Book. Mary would move, but not immediately, although the sovereign's intentions were widely known and either appreciated or feared. Cranmer, for a short time, remained Archbishop of Canterbury and not a few protestant-minded bishops were also in post. The Archbishop was permitted by Mary to conduct the funeral of her half-brother, Edward, in August, and in Westminster Abbey, according to the rites and Communion service of the 1552 Book. Mary herself did not attend, but rather ordered three days of requiems for her brother, celebrated by her Lord Chancellor-designate, Bishop Stephen Gardiner. By September, Cranmer, along with Hugh Latimer and Nicholas Ridley, was a prisoner in the Tower.

The unravelling of the reformation and a protestant liturgy would commence, and the Prayer Book ceased to be used in

England and Wales, whilst there would continue to be enthusiastic and defiant usage amongst the exiles in continental Europe. In respect of the return to the Catholic liturgy, Cuming notes:

> 'Mary's first step towards the restoration of the Catholic liturgy was to repeal all the Edwardine legislation, and restore the position as it was in the last year of Henry VIII.... Later in 1554 the full Sarum rite was restored, and the history of the Book of Common Prayer during the rest of Mary's reign must be sought outside England.'
> ('A History of Anglican Liturgy')

It is not too difficult to appreciate the welcome return of the Mass amongst the populace given that it was familiar and appreciated during the lifetime of many. With the exception of the introduction of the Order for Communion in 1548, it had only been six years since the death of Henry VIII and the reign of Catholic Mary, and when the Mass and the appropriate adornment of the parish churches was part and parcel of everyday life and living. Even the 1549 Prayer Book in Edward's reign was not that dissimilar to the Sarum Mass, and it had only been within the previous year prior to Mary's accession that the full impact of a protestant reformation would have had any real experience and impact.

Although her reign began hopefully, and many thought religioun settled, following the turmoil under the reign of her brother, the clock would be put back to the settlement achieved by her father: Catholicism in name and practice but without the authority of the Pope, Edwards notes that:

> 'She was in a number of ways her father's daughter, and many of those who supported her against Queen Jane trusted that she would revive her father's religious policy. Until December 1554 she did exercise a supremacy over the Church while securing the repeal of the Protestant legislation passed in her brother's reign. Her

coronation titles included "Supreme Head of the Church"; a secret
dispensation arrived from Rome permitting this for the time being.'
('Christian England Volume 2: From the Reformation to the
18th Century')

There were two events during Mary's reign that caused doubt
and disillusion, if not despair, amongst the people concerning
her rule and thereby her religious reforms and requirements.
These were her marriage to King Philip II of Spain, a traditional
military competitor and enemy to England, and the public mass
burnings of those who retained their adherence to and practice
of the Protestant religion.

In respect of the marriage, Edwards writes:

'The mere prospect of this Spanish match ended Mary's honeymoon
with her people'
('Christian England Volume 2: From the Reformation to the
18th Century')

Philip and Mary married on 25th July, 1554 in Winchester
Cathedral, the ceremony being conducted by Bishop Gardiner,
who had already officiated at the coronation. Although Gardiner
saw advantages in a union with the House of Hapsburg, the
marriage was forlorn. Philip was eleven years Mary's junior and
her phantom pregnancy caused not only the king frustration and
impatience, not least when Mary entered a considerable period
of depression and decline, but also his boredom with the
English. There was little love for Spain amongst the English, and
Philip was the icon of the distrusted Spanish and represented the
challenge of Spain to England's increasing naval supremacy. He
left England in August 1555, only returning for three months
during 1557. Significant damage had already been done to
Mary's popularity and the religious reforms she introduced by
the marriage. There was to be no heir to the English throne, and

the whole affair forced a realisation upon the people that the successor to the declining and ill queen would be her half-sister, the protestant Elizabeth. The pragmatism of the English, although having welcomed the restoration of the Mass, recognised the immanence of the restoration of the Prayer Book, in some form. At least, the uncertainties produced by the Spanish dalliance would be replaced with both political and religious stability, if not settlement. Clergy and people would have to return to the Prayer Book in the near future, following the demise of the ailing Queen Mary.

The public burnings of those unable and unwilling to give up the Protestant faith in favour of Catholic practices and the return to the Mass provoked a revulsion and a sympathy for those who later were to be deemed martyrs. Whilst an execution by burning was never going to be a pleasant observance, the often horrific nature through a lack of sufficient wood, slowness of the fire and the display of righteous approval on the part of Church officials did very little to commend the Church to the ordinary person. Furthermore, although the distinction might not seem particularly relevant, the fact of former Church leaders, including bishops and Cranmer himself, being publicly burnt to death added to the shock and horror of the policy and practice. Duffy observes:

> 'For the regime, there was a delicate balance of advantage and danger to be weighed in the publicity surrounding the trials and burnings. Public executions of the protestant hard core were seen as an essential manifestation of the determination and irreversibility of the government's commitment to the catholic restoration....The Queen gave specific instructions that Bishop Hooper was to be burned in Gloucester, "for the example and terror of suche as he hath there seduced and mistaught, and bycause he hath moste harme there"'

('Fires of Faith: Catholic England under Mary Tudor')

The death of Mary and the anticipated accession of Elizabeth, including thereby the restoration of the Prayer Book, would become an accepted understanding on the religious and liturgical landscape. This acceptance was enhanced by the departure of King Philip, the barrenness of the queen, the burnings of protestants, and the subsequent return of the exiles, including leading churchmen from the Edwardine period, armed with their 1552 Prayer Books, and some with hopes of further reform influenced by continental practice.

It has been the contention of this book that Bishop Hooper and others of a similar Zwinglian persuasion were the chief architects of the 1552 Book, rather than Cranmer himself. The particularly cruel and botched roasting of Hooper was a defining moment for reformation principles, and many turned out to witness the barbarism, mostly perhaps because it was market day in Gloucester. Again, Duffy records that:

'The burning of a bishop for heresy was an event without precedent in English history and Hooper, the most abrasive of new brooms, had been a controversial and, in many quarters, an unpopular bishop in both his midland dioceses.'
('Fires of Faith: Catholic England under Mary Tudor')

The matter concerning Thomas Cranmer's interrogation and subsequent burning would have further induced not just a sense of sympathy for the man who had been leader of the English Church, as Archbishop of Canterbury, since 1533, but a degree of familiarity and possible respect for one who had not only assisted in ridding the country from the authority of the Pope, but had also spearheaded an English liturgy that was available and accessible to all. Furthermore, the services and ceremonies of the Church as contained within the 1549 Prayer Book were to be found in a single volume that was both affordable and accessible to the laity. At a time when the English nation was finding and establishing a significant identity throughout the known world, an English Church, using the English language, under the authority of the monarch was an integral part of English self-esteem, which would match the previous hegemony of the French and Spanish nations. The power and influence of the Holy Roman Emperor was also challenged by the English Reformation, although a different impact was experienced within the German territories.

Thomas Cranmer was initially put on trial for treason in London on charges of helping to seize the Tower for Queen Jane and of levying troops for Northumberland's force against Mary. However, although punishable by death, Mary sought a conviction for what she considered the greater offence of heresy, MacCulloch suggests that:

> '.... whatever satisfaction the Queen might gain from seeing him die immediately for treason.... he had committed a far more serious crime: he had led the whole realm into heresy. He must die for that, but only after due trial.'
>
> ('Thomas Cranmer')

Cranmer's pragmatism and fair weathered approach was perhaps exemplified in his initial recantations of his previous protestant position when interrogated by a number of officials, scholars and churchmen. There can be little doubt that Cranmer, having witnessed the burnings of Ridley and Latimer, was profoundly afraid of his own possible fate. Whilst not analogous, it would appear that Cranmer's position concerning the reform of the 1549 Prayer Book was also one of compliance with the drift and reality of the prevailing wind of opinion and which might secure his own well-being and position. Cleary the recantations were a political and theological coup for the new regime and order. However, it had already been determined that Cranmer was to be executed at the stake. Dr Henry Cole, in the final confrontation with Cranmer in the Church of St Mary the Virgin, Oxford had the task in his sermon, which was originally to have been given beside the stake if weather had permitted, of explaining why a repentant sinner should still be burnt for heresy. He had little choice but to admit the problem from canon law, but found biblical justification in King David's acceptance of punishment for his sins.

However, Cranmer's position now changed significantly when he abjured his recantations. Cranmer did not follow the agreed text and stated publicly that his writings were written 'contrary to the truth which I thought in my heart, and written for fear of death' and consisted of 'all such bills and papers which I have written or signed with my hand since my degradation'. There was the inevitable commotion and anger, Cranmer being physically pulled down from the pulpit. He knew his death was inevitable, and it is recorded that as the flames consumed his body, he fulfilled a promise he had made in his last shouts in the church, 'forasmuch as my hand offended, writing contrary to my heart, my hand shall first be punished there-for'. He repeated these words for as long as he could, stretching out his hand into the heart of the fire.

This was indeed drama of a horrific but moving nature. It was also a significant error on the part of the queen and her advisers. Duffy writes:

> *'The decision to execute Cranmer despite six recantations was a major tactical error, for which the Queen was probably responsible. A living and penitent Cranmer would have been a huge propaganda asset for the regime: dead, he gave evangelicals an inspiring martyr.'*

('Fires of Faith: Catholic England under Mary Tudor')

The inspiration and affection, if not pity that Cranmer was held in by the English people, even in spite of their attraction to the religious order of Henry VIII, and with which he was associated, was inevitably linked to an English Prayer Book. Was this, however, the 1549 Book, which was perceived as the work of Cranmer, as opposed to the overtly protestant Book of 1552?

We shall see.

Chapter Seven

Off to 1559, 1604 and 1662

Henry VIII's daughter with Anne Boleyn, Elizabeth, ascended to the throne upon the death of her half-sister, Mary, in 1558. Without doubt, given the issues concerning Mary's reign, and identified in the previous chapter, there was a sense of relief that there would not only be a new and different regime, but that there would be stability, both in terms of social order, and an acceptable religious settlement. Whilst it was readily understood and appreciated that the settlement would be Protestant, there was uncertainty and ambiguity as to what precise form such would take. Many were aware that Elizabeth's religious and spiritual outlook was more reflective of the Henrician settlement than that as represented by the latter years of her half-brother's reign, and the 1552 Prayer Book. Elizabeth was in no rush just to re-institute, let alone enforce this book. On 27th December, 1558, a little over a month since she became queen, Elizabeth issued a proclamation prohibiting any change in the existing religious order, "until consultation may be had by Parliament". Cranmer was now dead, so there clearly could be no direct influence by the former archbishop upon any religious settlement or polity, although the question remains that if the 1549 Prayer Book was Cranmer's definitive work, rather than that of 1552, and if the former book was more indicative of the new queen's personal preference, then his legacy would endure into the new reign.

Elizabeth, however, had considerable pressure to both re-issue through a new Act of Uniformity the usage of the 1552 Book, not least from the rapidly returning exiles for whom the book had been a sustaining influence and identity within continental Europe, and for those who had been subject to the teachings and preaching of the likes of John Knox and John

Calvin, to abandon the Prayer Book in favour of the Genevan Form of Prayers. Cuming notes:

'The queen must have realized that, if she did not accept the 1552 Book, she would face a demand for the Genevan "Form of Prayers"'
('A History of Anglican Liturgy')

Elizabeth was also under considerable pressure to express her views and preference. The Prayer Book exiles clearly demanded a simple restitution of the 1552 Book in its entirety and without alteration. Those exiles who were influenced by a more reformed and extreme Protestantism, and had been using a liturgy that departed from the Prayer Book in significant ways, were advocating and articulating a drastic alteration to the Prayer Book, and most especially symbols and vesture that they identified with a residual form of popery and repugnance. Elizabeth was very minded to secure a peaceful settlement, not least for the stability of the kingdom. In acknowledging that the origins of what was to become the 1559 Prayer Book has been much debated, Jeanes observes that:

'It is clear that compromise between traditionalists and evangelicals was impossible. If a new book based on 1549 was considered (and there is evidence that Elizabeth was attracted to it), the Marian bishops were implacably opposed. They had been there under Edward and were not going there again. Not that Elizabeth had great affection for the Catholic establishment that had condemned her as illegitimate; but nor did she warm to the Marian exiles returning with their ideas for more advanced reform. John Knox in Geneva had written against "the monstrous regiment of women", meaning Mary, but the book ended his career in Elizabeth's England.'
('The Tudor Prayer Books' in 'Comfortable Words: Polity, Piety and The Book of Common Prayer')

It was clear that much was both expected and hoped for in the first months of Elizabeth's reign. Whilst it was also clear that there would be no return to the Catholic Mass and obedience to Rome, those of a Catholic disposition looked to a settlement that would predate the 1552 Prayer Book, and would either establish the form of the Mass as evidenced in the final years of her father's reign, or, failing that, the re-introduction of the 1549 Prayer Book which represented and articulated many Catholic principles. On the other hand, there were the two opposing and opposed protestant constituencies seeking either a restitution of the 1552 Book or, for others, a form of the Genevan Service Book. Elizabeth, desperate to unite her kingdom, was between a rock and a hard place. Davies suggests that:

'(t)he Liturgy was for Queen Elizabeth the way to maintain religious uniformity in her realm, a political mechanism for the manufacturing of loyalty.'
('Worship and Theology in England: From Cranmer to Hooker 1534-1603')

On 18th March, 1559 a Bill was brought into Parliament providing that 'no persons shall be punished for using the religion used in King Edward's last year'. This represented the consultation Elizabeth had promised in December, 1558. At the end of April, 1559 an Act of Uniformity was passed. Annexed to it was the Prayer Book of 1552 with a few small but important alterations. It would appear that this represented the middle ground that Elizabeth felt necessary to adopt, even if such was not entirely representative of her own position and opinion. Cranmer's 1549 Book had been superseded by that of Hooper, Zwingli, and others of the Zurich Reformation within the 1552 Book. However, the changes made, and which most certainly would have been articulated by Elizabeth, were not without significance. Cuming summarises these:

'Papal Catholics were placated by the omission of references to the Bishop of Rome and his "detestable enormities" in the Litany......Adherents of 1549 were encouraged by the restoration of the Words of Administration from that book, which were now combined with those of 1552; by the quiet dropping of the "Black Rubric" on kneeling at communion; and by a new rubric prefixed to Morning Prayer, directing the use of "such ornaments in the church as were in use by authority of Parliament in the second year of the reign of King Edward the Sixth".'

('A History of Anglican Liturgy')

The Words of Administration from 1549 would clearly have been interpreted in a Catholic way as indicative of the real presence of Christ within the sacrament, whilst the following words, if all recited together, would suggest a presence only appropriated by faith and in remembrance. The Black Rubric was a late insertion, hence black rather than red, into 1552 in order to placate John Knox and his exception to kneeling as suggesting both real presence and adoration. The Ornaments Rubric would appear to indicate the retention and use of ornaments and vestments that reflected a Catholic presentation of worship and especially the Eucharist. The rubric was to form the basis of much debate and practice concerning ritual in the Church of England in the late nineteenth century and beyond.

Whilst Elizabeth retained the crucifix and candles within the Chapel Royal, to the dislike of many of her supporters, other regal instructions, whilst giving a nod to some protestant insistencies, nevertheless retained, at least for the time being certain catholic practices. Jeanes notes that:

'(t)he Royal Injunctions of 1559 provided for the orderly removal of stone altars and their replacement by a communion table. But other clauses of the Injunctions sounded conservative, even reactionary, reinstating the Rogationtide procession around the parish and

requiring wafer bread for the Communion. This created an ensemble totally contrary to the spirit of the evangelical Reformers: the Communion celebrated by a priest in medieval vestments using not ordinary bread but a form of loaf reminiscent of the host in the Mass......Resistance was immediate and determined.'
('The Tudor Prayer Books' in 'Comfortable Words: Polity, Piety and The Book of Common Prayer')

Elizabeth's own position and desires for the liturgy was sacrificed on the altar of protestant resistance to any change from that represented by the 1552 Prayer Book, and those who could use any indication of the Catholic Mass or even the 1549 Prayer Book as weapons to challenge or even attack the queen. The English Reformation as expressed in the prayer books of Edward VI, and driven by Archbishop Cranmer, was not going to effect the uniformity desired for an English Church under the sovereignty of a godly monarch. It could be argued that the book of 1549 would have achieved both uniformity, accord and reconciliation between contrasting theologies and ecclesiologies if it were not for the influences and political engagements of those of a Zwinglian disposition, together with the concomitant power over Edward VI by such as Seymour and Northumberland. For all Elizabeth's attempts at reconciliation and the restitution of the 1552 Prayer Book, there was going to be continued discord and dispute both within the Established Church and those outside, whether Catholic or Puritan. The tensions and controversy would continue into the reign of Elizabeth's successor, James VI of Scotland and James I of England in 1603.

The accession of James represented for the first time in nearly a century no change of religion. However, previous issues and controversies were still very much present, albeit beneath the surface of loyalty and religious practice and observance. Towards the end of Elizabeth's reign, Edwards suggests that:

'It was by now the generally agreed Puritan policy to await the Queen's death and her replacement by a more "godly" successor from a securely Protestant Scotland.'

('Christian England Volume 2: From the Reformation to the 18ᵗʰ Century')

The Puritans, seeking further reform and significant amendment to the Prayer Book, wasted little time following James' journey south from Scotland. They presented what is known as the Millenary Petition, articulating concerns and seeking the new king's support for change. James followed precedent and summoned a conference to consider the issues raised before producing a new edition of the Prayer Book. Whilst the king neither accepted nor rejected the petition, the matter came under discussion at the conference held at Hampton Court in January, 1604. Eight suggestions were made and enjoined by the king in a proclamation prefixed to the Prayer Book, although even these were limited by the bishops prior to publication. The only significant and lasting decision made was to instruct a new translation of the Bible, which was completed in 1611 and known colloquially as the King James' Bible. Beckwith notes that:

'The English Prayer Book of 1604 made no alteration in the Elizabethan Communion service.'

('The Anglican Eucharist: From the Reformation to the Restoration' in 'The Study of Liturgy')

The legacy of Cranmer's 1549 Prayer Book disappears further into the mists of time, until, that is, 1637 in Scotland, and 1662 in England.

The Book of Common Prayer of 1662 has been regarded as the definitive liturgical book for the Church of England for some 350 years. It has also been described as the work of Thomas Cranmer, even one hundred years after his death. However, although based in large part, but with some amendments, on the 1604 Book of King James, there was a hiatus in 1637 with the attempt to impose not only an English liturgy upon Presbyterian inclined Scotland, but also one that in the main reverted to the 1549 Book. There had been moves throughout the reign of James by ecclesiastics such as Lancelot Andrewes, John Overall, John Cosin, Matthew Wren and William Laud to effect changes in the performance of the liturgy, and which could be identified with 1549. With the accession of Charles I in 1625, who was sympathetic to these changes, and William Laud becoming Archbishop of Canterbury, such moves were given added impetus. However, it was to become all too clear as to the resistance to these developments within a country that only twenty years previous had foiled a Catholic inspired attempt to overthrow the king and parliament in what became known as the Gunpowder Plot, and what was construed as papist incursions into a Protestant liturgy. The main influence on the 1637 Scottish Book was Bishop Wedderburn of Dunblane and the attempt to impose the Book had significant consequences beyond even that of liturgical reform. Hannah Cleugh observes that:

'(t)his reached crisis point when Laud attempted to impose a new Prayer Book (referred to as "Laud's Liturgy") on the Scottish Church in 1637, which led the following year to the Solemn League and Covenant against the Prayer Book and to the outbreak of war in the Three Kingdoms'
('The Prayer Book in Early Stuart Society' in 'Comfortable Words: Polity, Piety and The Book of Common Prayer')

The book was quickly dropped, for as Cuming notes:

'To the Scots the book reeked of popery......Little as they liked the Prayer Book, they were highly sensitive to any change in its text.'
('A History of Anglican Liturgy')

A further hiatus in the life of the Prayer Book now occurred with the Civil War, the execution of both Laud and Charles I, the ascendancy of the Puritans and the prevailing desire for further liturgical reforms along Puritan lines. The Puritans had been discontent since the reign of Elizabeth, and many of their hopes and desires remained unfulfilled. Now was their moment, and such went beyond wanting a revision of the Prayer Book. In January 1645 the use of the Prayer Book was declared illegal and it was replaced by 'A Directory of Public Worship of God'. It was not so much a text, but rather a series of suggestions and directions. Cuming notes that:

> '(t)he Lord's Day Service follows the tradition of Bucer, Calvin, and Knox, with an occasional concession to the more radical Independents, who were now asserting themselves against the moderate Puritans, or Presbyterians.'

('A History of Anglican Liturgy')

Whether Cranmer was responsible for the Prayer Book of 1552 and thereby its successors of 1559 and 1604, this liturgical inheritance was now buried and lost for the time being. However, such was the affection of many that ways were found of using the Book, and there was a certain amount of clandestine use of the Ordinal. Not all was lost, and many beneficed clergy were able to use the Directory in a Prayer Book manner. As with the Marian exiles, the use of the Prayer Book retained what for many represented the continuation of the essential element of the English Reformation, within the context of a regime and religious programme and policy that was significantly different from what had been both fought for and deeply treasured. There was perhaps also a suspicion, if not antipathy to what was perceived as continental forms that were alien to English comprehensiveness, which was regarded as something represented by the Prayer Book. Not everyone, however, saw it in such terms.

It was apparent that with the death of the Protector, Oliver Cromwell, and the dissatisfaction with his son, Richard, the return of the executed Charles I's son, also Charles, was both a necessary development, and for many a most welcome one. Even Cromwell, at one point, had opined that it was difficult to imagine England without a king. Charles Stuart was to return from exile in Breda after having promised a general pardon and religious toleration pending a permanent settlement by Parliament. On the same day that this declaration was received, the House of Commons voted that 'the government is, and ought to be, by King, Lords and Commons'. By the end of May, 1660, Charles had been proclaimed king and had landed at Dover.

Whilst he was rapturously welcomed, all was by no means settled or assured in terms of a religious settlement which focused upon bishops and the Prayer Book. There was further confusion concerning Charles personal religious position, and there were suggestions that he had converted to Roman Catholicism during the exile. What was not in doubt was his marriage, like his late father, to a Catholic princess. For the present purpose, the issue concerns the use and possible restoration of the Prayer Book which, if reformed, may incorporate aspects of the 1549 Book, which was clearly Cranmerian, or perhaps just a re-affirmation and imposed use of the 1552 Book, as modified in 1559 and 1604, but perhaps not the primary work of Cranmer. Charles was only too well aware of the differences of religious views and positions within his kingdom, together with the Scottish issue concerning the 1637 Book and a well-established Presbyterian order. Edwards notes:

'When Charles II exchanged pious remarks with Presbyterian ministers on his return to London, it therefore seemed possible that government of the Church by bishops would be forgotten. After all, the estates confiscated from the bishops and their cathedrals were now in lay hands.'

('Christian England Volume 2: From the Reformation to the 18th Century')

Change to the Prayer Book was once again the fashion as opportunity presented itself with the Restoration. There was little doubt that the Church of England would return to the Book of Common Prayer as its defined and defining liturgy and ecclesiology. However, what would be the form of a revised and authorised book, and what changes might be either acceptable or even achievable? By 1660, and after the Commonwealth period, there were two contrasting challenges, whilst at the same time there was also a desire amongst some for no change to the Book of 1604. On the one hand, there were the Puritans, who were, in the main, Presbyterians, who urged and hoped for a final removal from a formal liturgy those items which they had long resisted as being Papist, and reflecting what they perceived as a still unpurged Catholic rite with little place in a reformed Church. In contrast to this school were those who sought a liturgy that reflected the practices and examples of the Caroline divines, including the much loved and respected Lancelot Andrewes, represented not just within the 1549 Book but also, and with an element of political discretion, that of the rejected Scottish Book of 1637. It is possible that this constituency was the true heir to the ideals of Thomas Cranmer in their desire for a liturgy that was both dignified, whilst Catholic and Reformed. The restored king would have to give due consideration to both these traditions, who were not without influence, as well as recognising the pressure just to restore matters to their pre-Commonwealth position.

The Savoy Conference began on 15th April, 1661, under the chairmanship of the Bishop of London, Gilbert Sheldon, to consider possible alterations to the Book of Common Prayer, which was that of 1604. The two sides were represented by, on the one hand, Richard Baxter, vicar of Kidderminster, for the Presbyterians, and Bishops John Cosin and Matthew Wren were the plaintiffs for a more Catholic amendment. Beckwith identifies the two parties:

> *'The first consisted of the Presbyterians Puritans, who were hoping for a revision of the Prayer Book in the direction of their own current practice. At the Savoy Conference (1661) they put their proposals to the bishops in two forms: (i) detailed suggestions for change in the 1604 text, to which the bishops replied; (ii) a completely different liturgy drawn up by Richard Baxter, which was virtually ignored. The second group consisted primarily of two surviving Laudian bishops, Cosin and Wren, to whom the credit for the 1662 revision has often been ascribed.'*

('The Anglican Eucharist to the Restoration' in 'The Study of Liturgy')

However, given not only the rejection of the majority of Presbyterian suggestions, but also the limited changes to the 1604 text, it is hard to argue that Cosin and Wren achieved a great deal. It was not, however, for the want of trying. Cuming points out that the two bishops, in preparation for the review:

> *'.... combined their suggestions in the volume called the "Durham Book", a Prayer Book dated 1619 in which Cosin entered the bulk of alterations and additions proposed by himself and Wren......Most notably, whereas neither had previously so much as mentioned the Scottish Liturgy, it is quite obvious that they now had it open on the table in front of them.'*

('A History of Anglican Liturgy')

For our present purpose, suffice it to acknowledge that the Savoy Conference produced very little of substance concerning change in either a Puritan or Catholic direction. The chairmanship of Bishop Sheldon was influential in conceding very little to either protagonists, recognising the possibility of continued discontent, and seeking a settlement with as little controversy as possible through a simple return to the *status quo ante*. However, the unity so desired, through an Act of Uniformity re-instating the Prayer Book in 1662, was not achieved. Cranmer's dream of a single rite, both Catholic and Reformed, through an English Prayer Book was to be quickly denied by subsequent requirements of conformity and submission. Susan Durber acknowledges that:

> *'Very quickly it was clear that something like the former Prayer Book was about to be imposed once more and there was little patience for a longer period of discussion that might well have saved the unity of the Church .... Any who did not conform would be deprived of their livings or indeed of their posts as school teachers or heads of colleges. Thus did the Book of Common Prayer become a talisman of exclusion, as ten per cent of the clergy were ejected and English culture and society were radically split.'*

('Voices from the Rift' in 'Wrestling with a Godly Order: Encounters with the 1662 Book of Common Prayer')

In spite of this reality and the divisions of the seventeenth and eighteenth centuries, the 1662 Book has left an enduring mark upon the English liturgical scene that, although rejected within a variety of non-conformist ecclesial groups, has found admiration and a fondness that has transcended protestant divisions through to the present day. This is not just represented by the language of the Prayer Book, but also a recognition of a unifying effect within the Church of England and what emerged as the Anglican Church with a worldwide dimension and experience. Perhaps this could be Cranmer's legacy, even if the Communion rite did not accord with his initial excursion into liturgical reform. However, liturgical controversy was to break out again in the latter years of the nineteenth and early years of the twentieth centuries and which centred, in no small part, on interpretations of the 1662 Prayer Book and its use.

We shall see.

Chapter Eight

20th and 21st century legacies of just 3 years

The continued legacy of Cranmer and the Book of Common Prayer surfaced towards the end of the nineteenth century and the beginning of the twentieth, although rumblings of discontent emerged at the end of the eighteenth century and passed into the nineteenth. During this period, there was, in effect, only the 1662 version of the Prayer Book in use as the standard liturgy of the Church of England. Other Anglican Churches, in what were the colonies or part of the Empire, had begun to exercise their own liturgical liberation, reflecting both different and differing cultural and linguistic contexts. The dissatisfactions that had so bedevilled Prayer Book history in the sixteenth and seventeenth centuries were once more creating ecclesiological controversies. These were not so much concerning the text itself, but rather interpretations of meaning and usage. Whereas it would be true to suggest that the Evangelical Movement of the late eighteenth and early nineteenth centuries had sought, exhibited and expressed a greater emphasis on liturgical flexibility, not least through extra-liturgical events and services, there was a loyalty to the Prayer Book as the standard form of worship, and which survived into the eruption of Methodist practice and ecclesiastical separation. The Oxford Movement from 1833, on the other hand, although not initially concerned with liturgical issues and reform, nevertheless in affirming the catholicity of the Church of England, and in challenging prevailing and lax worship practices, gave rise to increased worship variation and ritualistic insertions into the Prayer Book liturgy. Key amongst subsequent developments were an appeal to the Ornaments Rubric and the tradition as represented by the 1549 and 1637 Prayer Books. The

Ornaments Rubric was the centre of much argument and controversy. It stated:

> 'And here is to be noted, that such ornaments of the Church, and of
> the Ministers thereof at all times of their ministration, shall be
> retained, and be in use, as were in this Church of England by the
> authority of Parliament in the second year of the reign of King
> Edward VI.'

We are immediately drawn back to the 1549 Prayer Book and its
continued influence on liturgical interpretation. Cuming
suggests that:

> 'The first question at issue was the meaning of 'second year' of
> Edward VI: was this before or after the publication of the Book of
> 1549? If before, then the full medieval range of vestments and
> furnishings was legal; if after, those at any rate that were mentioned
> in the Book were legal.'

('A History of Anglican Liturgy')

From the time of the Oxford Movement, dated from John Keble's
Assize Sermon in the University Church of St Mary the Virgin,
Oxford on 14th July, 1833, and the continued influence of the
Tractarians, even after some notable departures to the Church of
Rome, ritualistic practices and the adornment of parish churches
in the Church of England were increasingly evidenced in the
middle years of the nineteenth century. For many, both ritualists
and those opposing the changes and innovations within the
Established Church, the lightening rod was the Ornaments
Rubric immediately preceding the Order for Morning Prayer in
the Book of Common Prayer. Joyce Coombs writes in her book
about Father Arthur Tooth, vicar of St James', Hatcham, 1868-
1877, and the first priest to be imprisoned for ritual practices
under the Public Worship Regulation Act, 1874:

'Most important of all, the use of ritual and ornaments began to acquire a new significance, and became entangled with doctrinal questions......these had been no more than adjuncts of worship, albeit primitive and aesthetic ones, which had fallen into disuse, and were sanctioned, so it seemed, by rubrics in the Book of Common Prayer.'
('Judgement on Hatcham: The History of a Religious Struggle 1877-1886')

The passing of the Public Regulation Worship Act in 1874, ostensibly to regulate and restrict ritualistic practices, gave rise to a resistance to a piece of legislation passed by what was deemed a secular parliament, with many non-churchmen and non-Christian members, in contradiction to what was seen as the tradition of the Church and various judgements made by the Church concerning worship practices. There was strong episcopal support, with some notable exceptions, for the Act as bishops, in the face of parochial complaints and social disorder, resulting occasionally in violence, and in order to ensure compliance with episcopal direction and the law. Five members of the clergy were imprisoned under the Act, which resulted in increased ambivalence about the Act and its implications. For many within the Catholic tradition in the Church of England, these priests were martyrs. The Evangelical Lord Shaftsbury described the use of Eucharistic vestments as the 'marks of the Romish Mass and the Romish priesthood, and must be eliminated'. The struggles of the sixteenth century and Prayer Book reform are being visited upon the latter half of the nineteenth century.

Whilst not urging or advocating reform of the Prayer Book, there was a usage, or in some instances a conscious non-usage, that gave tangible and visual evidence of interpretations that were clearly other than just a plain reciting of the Prayer Book text. There were, of course, those who were not affected by either the Evangelical or Catholic movements, and who saw and had no inclination to change current liturgical expression in the worship of the Parish Church. However, it would not be long before all Churches were affected by developments in one way or another.

For the present purpose of discerning the influence of Thomas Cranmer, it needs to be noted that within the Catholic trajectory his early sixteenth century reforms were those that were to exert the most impact. There can be little doubt that the reforms and the amendments that those of the Catholic disposition within the Church, further to the Oxford Movement and the emergent of those known as Tractarians, were to make were based, in large part, upon the text and structure of the 1549 Book. Hylson-Smith observes that those who were also known as of the High Church disposition:

> ' ..... although High Churchmen ...... differed from Evangelicals in admitting to a preference for the communion service in the first Prayer Book of King Edward VI, over the amended version of 1552 which removed those features which were most strongly suggestive of the sacrifice of the mass and the real presence of Christ in the sacrament, this did not become a "hot" issue until it became associated with what were seen as Romeward trends among the Tractarians.'

('The Churches in England from Elizabeth 1 to Elizabeth 11: Volume 11 1689-1833')

Apart from ritual insertions, including what were to become common practice in most Church of England parishes, such as the use of crosses, candles, the eastward position for the celebration of the Eucharist, the changes wished for and often implemented without authority, were of structure in the position of parts of the liturgy and the inclusion of forms only previously present in the 1549 Book. In many respects it was like putting 1552 into reverse. The use of the traditional mass vestments, incense and reservation of the Sacrament were evidenced only in what were known as the more extreme or advanced churches of Anglo-Catholicism. The main points of reversion to a form not unlike 1549 included the re-positioning of the Gloria in Excelsis to its place at the beginning of the liturgy, the use of the Kyries, responses to the proclamation of the Gospel, the movement of the Prayer of Oblation to immediately follow what was known as the Prayer of Consecration and before the communion, and the reciting of the Agnus Dei. As well as reflecting an earlier form of worship, which many believed the 1549 Book represented, it was clear that there was a general mood for liturgical change and revision, as well as the more specific one of having a rite that demonstrated overtly a celebration of a real presence of Christ within the Eucharistic elements. The movement of the Prayer of Oblation was a deliberate attempt to re-create the canon of the mass, and to emphasise the offering of Christ within the anaphora, rather than just an offering of the people after reception of communion. Bradshaw and Johnson draw attention to this concerning 1552:

'...... and what had been the final part of the eucharistic prayer was deferred until after communion to become a prayer of oblation by those made worthy to offer themselves and their praise through their reception of the bread and wine.'

('The Eucharistic Liturgies: Their evolution and interpretation')

This is a clear reference to the significant theological change represented by the 1552 Book compared to that of 1549, and the re-positioning seeks to return to a more Catholic interpretation of the Eucharist and perhaps, thereby, more in accordance with the view of Cranmer prior to and immediately subsequent to 1549.

The impetus for liturgical reform was driven not just by the increased use of ritual and ceremony, although such had resulted in the Public Regulation of Worship Act, 1874 and the imprisonment of a number of clergy. Together with the use of the Act and the accusation made against the 'saintly' Bishop Edward King of Lincoln for practices now commonplace, there was reluctance to press such matters further. However, it was thought that compromises could be reached by a reform of the Prayer Book that would permit certain practices, restrict others but, above all, function with legal and episcopal authority. This resulted in a Royal Commission in 1904 to inquire into alleged instances of indiscipline in public worship. It stated:

'The law of public worship in the Church of England is too narrow for the religious life of the present generation. It needlessly condemns much which a great section of Church people, including many of her most devoted members, value; and modern thought and feelings are characterised by a care for ceremonial, a sense of dignity in worship, and an appreciation of the continuity of the Church, which were not similarly felt at the time when the law took its present shape.'

The Commission recommended that Letters of Business should be issued to the Convocations to consider a new ornaments rubric, and to frame changes to the existing law concerning worship. This led to the process which would lead to the finally rejected 1928 Prayer Book. Much has been written about this process and the various Books which were presented to parliament and which were not approved. Certain controversies were inevitable; the provision for the reservation of the consecrated elements, and the re-positioning of the Prayer of Oblation, amongst others, offended those of an Evangelical and Low Church persuasion; whilst, on the other hand, Catholics felt that restrictions concerning the reserved Sacrament were too limiting and there were objections to the epiclesis (the invocation of the

Holy Spirit) upon the elements of bread and wine after the recitation of the words of institution, which Catholics viewed as consecratory with no further suggestion of consecration. Beckwith observes, concerning reservation, the Prayer of Oblation and the epiclesis:

> 'It was these as much as any part of the book that moved extreme Evangelicals and extreme Anglo-Catholics to unite in opposition to the proposals. The first were opposed to any provision for reservation and the latter to the severe regulations preventing devotions and ceremonies surrounding it.
>
> Beside the reservation question, the position of the Prayer of oblation was the cause of bitter controversy …… (Bishop Frere) had advocated the re-introduction of the epiclesis into the service and had argued that the primitive Church regarded the whole consecration Prayer as consecratory and not any particular part of it.'
> ('The Anglican Eucharist to the Restoration' in 'The Study of Liturgy')

The final version of the Book was rejected by parliament (which raised its own issue as to the influence and power of parliament, containing those other than Anglicans or Christian, to have an imprimatur in matters of the Church of England), but was given episcopal authority for use, whilst not technically or legally replacing the 1662 Book. It was not until 1965 and the revision of the law enabling the Church to exercise greater freedom in the determination of its worship, that changes to the Prayer Book were permitted and made available through three series of worship booklets, prior to the production of an entire book in 1980 known as the Alternative Service Book (ASB). As with Series 1, 2 and 3 service booklets, the ASB, as its title suggests, was alternative to the Book of Common Prayer. The ASB eventually had a twenty-year shelf-life, to be replaced by Common Worship in 2000. The latter incorporated Prayer Book texts as well as an increased variety of optional Eucharistic prayers. The Church of England now possessed a single book which contained and reflected the variety of traditions and practices that had developed subsequent to 1549, but which also drew upon other sources from other liturgical traditions.

It would be fair to state that the legacy of Thomas Cranmer, alongside a variety of other material, survives and lives within Common Worship, even if there is a question as to whether that legacy is to be found primarily in the 1549 Prayer Book, or that of 1552. For the purpose of this book, that legacy resides primarily in the former, which was amended by others in just three years for political as well as theological purposes. Whether the result was satisfactory from a purely liturgical perspective is an open question. Clearly, the 1552 Book by virtue of historical timing, and changes in religious settlements, became loved and valued by exiles, both in the sixteenth and seventeenth centuries.

Conclusion

The prime purpose of this book is not to undermine or deny both the liturgical skills and the importance of Thomas Cranmer, Archbishop of Canterbury, during what most would recognise as being turbulent and even violent years of political and religious reform and settlement. There can be no doubt of Cranmer's creativity in reforms prior to the death of Henry VIII in 1547, the accession of Edward VI and the production of the first English Prayer Book of 1549. Cranmer was also a tried and tested skilled political maneuverer, steering liturgical and political paths through the vagaries and variations as represented by both monarchs and their agents and advisers. The fact that the standard liturgical text in the Church of England today continues to be the 1662 Book of Common Prayer, whether within its own volume or that of Common Worship, recognising the significant elements that came from 1549, and through the changes represented by the books of 1552, 1559 and 1604, is indicative of the legacy of and debt owed to Cranmer in the life and worship of the contemporary Church. Although the use and popularity of what are often, and perhaps incorrectly, called modern services in the life of the ordinary parish church, is often set alongside a continued usage of the Book of Common Prayer, not least at early Sunday celebrations. Cathedrals often maintain a Prayer Book usage, as do those clergy and parishes that will use no other. The Prayer Book lives, and Cranmer lives through its legal status and continued love and use.

The contention of this book is that Cranmer was responsible for the 1549 Prayer Book, but not directly that of the 1552 Prayer Book, produced just three years later. In addition to believing that he could have so significantly changed his mind as to the settlement of the English Reformation in so short a period of time, and the possibility that he was duplicitous in producing a rite for national use, knowing that churches and parishioners would shortly have to experience further turbulent changes in both the liturgy and the ordering of their churches, does not indicate a sensitivity of pastoral and responsible care for the English people. Cranmer, however, was both a supporter of the royal supremacy, and how could he be otherwise given his close involvement in establishing the same, which necessitated a certain subservience to the wishes of the king. However, he was also a pragmatist and would follow prevailing reformed principles that were in the ascendant. The influences of Ulrich Zwingli, as represented by John Hooper, Bishop of Gloucester, the second Protector, the Duke of Northumberland, John Bullinger, Martin Bucer and other continental reformers, and the king himself would weaken any resistance Cranmer might have wished against the significant changes proposed to the 1549 Book, resulting in that of 1552. In many respects, Cranmer's language, prayers and cadences survived this more avowedly protestant upheaval, whilst the structure, order and theology of his 1549 Book was decimated. Even the support of the arch-conservative, Stephen Gardiner, Bishop of Winchester, would not save 1549, and possibly acted as a spur to those seeking a further reformation. Bradshaw and Johnson note:

'Within three years, however, a second Book of Common Prayer was produced and replaced the first from All Saints' Day 1552. Scholars are divided over whether Cranmer had planned this version from the outset, always intending the 1549 Book to serve merely as an interim measure to introduce the process of reform, or whether this later book only came into being as a reaction to certain conservative bishops – among them Stephen Gardiner, bishop of Winchester, who found that the first book was just about compatible with Catholic teaching – and under pressure for more radical reform from the likes of John Hooper, bishop of Gloucester.'

('The Eucharistic Liturgies: Their evolution and interpretation')

The debate as to Cranmer's involvement in the 1552 Prayer Book will no doubt continue, and scholars will without doubt disagree as to the level of that involvement, and if proved, how such came about within just three years. This book advocates a reluctant involvement to the extent that the re-ordering and re-wording of 1549 to produce 1552 was not of Cranmer's doing or wish, but that he accepted, possibly reluctantly, the trajectory of the English Reformation under the positive influences of Zwinglian disciples, and the negative impact of conservatives, such as Stephen Gardiner, who had no wish for any further changes than those set forth in the 1549 Book. The principle of an English Prayer Book, duly authorised, and Cranmerian words and phrases remained, to a large extent. However, there could have been no doubt that the 1552 Book was most definitely protestant, although there was a significant minority who could not accept even this analysis, and that the English Church was the child of the Zurich Reformation as opposed to that represented by Luther or even Calvin. It could further be argued that had it not been for the return to Catholicism under Queen Mary, and the burnings and exiles of protestant reformers and leading Church people with the usage and affection for 1552, the accession of Queen Elizabeth, whenever that might have been, could possibly have seen further reform of the Prayer Book, but in a more Catholic direction.

How much influence, if any, therefore, did Thomas Cranmer have upon the 1552 Prayer Book and the theology upon which it was based, is likely to be an ongoing question. It seems unlikely, however, that having produced such a liturgy as 1549, which clearly was both Catholic and Reformed, and which more than likely was in accord with the majority of English people, who had experienced a religious upheaval of significant proportions, that Cranmer would inflict further liturgical and theological disruption for the sake of pacifying the vagaries and variations of continental Protestantism.

Perhaps we shall never see!

About the Author

Canon David Jennings obtained a Bachelor of Divinity degree at Kings' College, London and a Master of Philosophy degree in marketing from the Business School at Loughborough University. He was ordained in Worcester Cathedral and served his title as curate in the parish of Halesowen. From there he went to be director of the project All Faiths for One Race in Handsworth, Birmingham, working with the late Rev Professor John Hick. He was also assistant priest in the parish of Holy Trinity, Birchfield. Canon Jennings then became the Bishop of Leicester's community relations officer and priest-in-charge of the parish of Snibston, in the diocese of Leicester. From 1987 until retirement in 2014, Canon Jennings was Rector of the parish of Burbage with Aston Flamville. He has held a number of positions in the diocese of Leicester, including chair of the Diocesan Evangelism Committee, chair of the Diocesan Board for Social Responsibility, chair of the Celebrate 80 Committee and Project Officer for Church and Society. He was made an Honorary Canon of Leicester Cathedral in 2003 and Canon Theologian in 2010, a position he continues to hold in addition to being a member of the Cathedral Chapter.

Canon Jennings has also been a local authority councillor and has chaired the council's Policy Committee. He has founded and chaired a number of voluntary organisations. For three years he was a member of the government sponsored National Consumer Council, representing the poor and disadvantaged. Until 1988 he was a partner in the family wholesale newsagent's business. Canon Jennings has been a regular broadcaster on BBC Radio Leicester, appearing on the BBC TV programme, the Big Question, and other television programmes. He continues to exercise an active priestly ministry within the diocese of Leicester.

He has written many articles and published lectures in his book, Rector's Reflections (Burbage Parish Church, 2014). Other publications include Power, Press Barons and the Harlot: the influence of the British press socially and politically 1920-1940 (Burbage Parish Church, 2011) and What's Still Right with the Church of England: a future for the Church of England (Circle Books, 2013).

Bibliography

Bellenger, D.A. & Fletcher, S., *The Mitre & the Crown: A History of the Archbishops of Canterbury.* Sutton, 2005

Bradshaw, P.F., Johnson, M. E., *The Eucharistic Liturgies: Their evolution and interpretation.* SPCK, 2012

Coombs, J., *Judgement on Hatcham: The History of a Religious Struggle 1877-1886.* The Faith Press, 1969

Cuming, G.J., *A History of Anglican Liturgy.* Macmillan, 1969

Davies, H., *Worship and Theology in England: From Cranmer to Hooker 1534-1603.* Oxford, 1970

Eds. Dickens, A.G. & Carr, D., *The Reformation in England,* Edward Arnold, 1967

Duffy, E., *Fires of Faith: Catholic England under Mary Tudor.* Yale, 2009

Duffy, E., *The Stripping of the Altars.* Yale, 1992

Edwards, D.L., *Christian England Volume 2: From the Reformation to the 18th Century,* Collins, 1983

Francis, H.J., *A History of Hinckley.* W. Pickering & Sons, Ltd., 1930

Hylson-Smith, K., *The Churches in England from Elizabeth 1 to Elizabeth 11: Volume 11 1689-1833.* SCM Press, 1997

Eds. Jones, C., Wainwright, G., Yarnold, E., *The Study of Liturgy.* SPCK, 1978

MacCulloch, D., *Thomas Cranmer.* Yale, 1996

Eds. Platten, S., Woods, C., *Comfortable Words: Polity, Piety and The Book of Common Prayer.* SCM, 2012

Ed. Robinson, H., *Original Letters Relative to the English Reformation,* Two Volumes, Cambridge: Parker Society, 1846-1847

Ed. Rowell, G., *The English Religious Tradition and the Genius of Anglicanism.* Ikon Productions Ltd., 1992

Skidmore, C., *Edwards VI: The Lost King of England.* Weidenfeld & Nicolson, 2007

Ed. Steven, J., *Wrestling with a Godly Order: Encounters with the 1662 Book of Common Prayer.* Sarum College Press, 2015

Stevenson, K., *Eucharist and Offering.* Pueblo, 1986

Eds. Stevenson, K., Spinks, B., *The Identity of Anglican Worship.* Mowbray, 1991

Chronos Books is a historical non-fiction imprint. Chronos publishes real history for real people; bringing to life historical people, places and events in an imaginative, easy-to-digest and accessible way. We want writers of historical books, from ancient times to the Second World War, that will add to our understanding of people and events rather than being a dry textbook; history that passes on its stories to a generation of new readers.